Scripture Discussion Commentary 10

SCRIPTURE DISCUSSION COMMENTARY 10

*Series editor:* Laurence Bright

# Paul  I

| | |
|---:|:---|
| **Paul's theology** | *Duncan Macpherson* |
| **1 and 2 Thessalonians** | *Mervyn Davies* |
| **Galatians** | *Lionel Swain* |
| **Romans** | *Anthony Walker* |
| **Ephesians** | *Duncan Macpherson* |

**ACTA Foundation**

**Adult Catechetical Teaching Aids**

**Chicago, Illinois**

First published 1972
ACTA Foundation (Adult Catechetical Teaching Aids),
4848 N. Clark Street, Chicago, Illinois 60640

Nihil obstat: John M. T. Barton STD LSS  *Censor*
Imprimatur: + Victor Guazzelli  *Vicar General*
Westminster, 17 April 1972

2547

Library of Congress Catalog Number: 71–173033

ISBN 0 87946 009 1

This book is set in 12/14 pt Linotype Baskerville

Made and printed in Great Britain by
William Clowes & Sons, Limited
London, Beccles and Colchester

# Contents

v

# General Introduction

A few of the individual units which make up this series of biblical commentaries have already proved their worth issued as separate booklets. Together with many others they are now grouped together in a set of twelve volumes covering almost all the books of the old and new testaments—a few have been omitted as unsuitable to the general purpose of the series.

That purpose is primarily to promote discussion. This is how these commentaries differ from the others that exist. They do not cover all that could be said about the biblical text, but concentrate on the features most likely to get lively conversation going—those, for instance, with special relevance for later developments of thought, or for life in the church and world of today. For this reason passages of narrative are punctuated by sets of questions designed to get a group talking, though the text of scripture, helped by the remarks of the commentator, should have already done just that.

For the text is what matters. Individuals getting ready for a meeting, the group itself as it meets, should always have the bible centrally present, and use the commentary only as a tool. The bibliographies will help those wishing to dig deeper.

What kinds of group can expect to work in this way? Absolutely any. The bible has the reputation of being difficult, and in some respects it is, but practice quickly clears up a lot of initial obstacles. So parish groups of any kind can and should be working on it. The groups needn't necessarily already exist, it is enough to have a few like-minded friends and to care sufficiently about finding out what the bible means. Nor need they be very large; one family could be quite enough. High schools (particularly in the senior year), colleges and universities are also obvious places for groups to form. If possible they should everywhere be ecumenical in composition: though all the authors are Roman catholics, there is nothing sectarian in their approach.

In each volume there are two to four or occasionally more studies of related biblical books. Each one is self-contained; it is neither necessary nor desirable to start at the beginning and plough steadily through. Take up, each time, what most interests you—there is very little in scripture that is actually dull! Since the commentaries are by different authors, you will discover differences of outlook, in itself a matter of discussion. Above all, remember that getting the right general approach to reading the bible is more important than answering any particular question about the text—and that this approach only comes with practice.

Volume 10 contains a general introduction to Paul's theological ideas, his early letters to the Thessalonians, and the two letters, Galatians and Romans, in which he works out the relationship between judaism and christianity. Finally there is the letter to the Ephesians, probably written by a close follower of Paul's after his death.

L. B.

# The theology of St Paul

In order to understand the thought of any theologian it is first necessary to understand the man. No matter how great the grace received, grace still builds upon nature. God reveals himself to a man but this revelation has to be understood within that man's own terms of reference. Some of these terms of reference may be inherited, others are determined by cultural background, education, or by class interest.

Paul's background was dominated by two conflicting tendencies. First, there was Saul the pharisee, a militant member of a scrupulously orthodox and exclusive party of judaism. Secondly, there was Paul the Roman citizen, a cosmopolitan member of a comfortable provincial merchant class. The tension between these two tendencies were only to be reconciled after his conversion on the Damascus road.

## Paul of Tarsus

Tarsus was the capital of Cilicia; standing at the cross roads of Asia Minor it was an important city, both commercially and culturally. In Ac 21:39 Paul is represented as sharing in the very considerable civic pride of Tarsus. The phrase 'no mean city' appeared with the motto 'first, fairest and best' on the local coinage.

The religious scene at Tarsus was richly varied. The

ancient religion of Tarsus had to compete with the cult
of Adonis and mystery religions like mithraism. The cosmopolitan character of the city was conducive to religious
tolerance and the Jewish population were relatively pros-
perous and important members of the community.

The mediterranean world of the time had a largely
slave-based economy. The peasant class were impoverished
and many city dwellers were unemployed. Paul was a free
man, a Roman citizen, who had served his apprenticeship
in tent-making; a reasonably lucrative trade in a pros-
perous city. It seems likely, also, that only a family in comfortable circumstances could have afforded to send him to
Jerusalem to finish his studies. As far as class was concerned,
then, Paul was an educated member of the first century
middle class. As such he might have been expected to
identify his own interests and values with those of the
Roman empire. As a Jew he could never quite manage to
do this.

## Saul the Benjaminite

It was quite common for Jews to give their children two
names, one biblical, and the other a Greek name. Since
his family belonged to the tribe of Benjamin, his parents
called their son Saul after King Saul, also a Benjaminite.
In addition they gave him the Greek name Paul. Saul was
a keen student of the law in the pharisaic tradition ('as to
the law a pharisee'; Phil 3:5) and showed great promise
as a rabbinic scholar. ('I advanced in Judaism beyond
many of my own age among my people, so extremely
jealous was I for the traditions of my fathers' Gal 1:14).
His education in pharisaism was completed under the
tutorship of Gamaliel (Ac 22:3), one of the most prestig-
ious teachers of the school of Hillel and successor of the

Rabbi Hillel himself. The school of Hillel was much more liberal and tolerant than the rival school of Shammai. In Ac 5 : 34–39 Gamaliel is reported as exhorting the sanhedrin to practise this same tolerance towards the early church. However much influence Gamaliel may have had upon Saul in other ways Saul appears to have adopted a rather harsh attitude towards christianity.

## The theology of the pharisees and the theology of Paul

The pharisees were the most observant Jews of their time. The name *'pharisee'* (like the term 'christian') was originally coined by their enemies and means 'separated ones'. The pharisees made great efforts to keep not only the law of Moses, as written in the Pentateuch, but also the unwritten law which had grown up around it. The minute observance of the law was seen as a vital prerequisite for the coming of the messianic age. As one later saying has it 'If the Israelites observed one Sabbath as it should be observed the Son of David would come immediately' (Rabbi Levi, c 300). This great emphasis on the law meant that temple worship was really peripheral to their religious interests.

Politically less extreme than the zealots, the pharisees probably preferred Roman rule to the rule of the great rivals, the priestly party. Certainly they did not believe, as the zealots did, that the kingdom could come through force of arms. Nevertheless, they hated foreign domination and regarded it as a sacrilege which would have to be effaced before the kingdom could be established by God. At the right time the pharisees were ready to fight to this end.

As with orthodox Jews in modern times, the pharisees practised a life style which marked them out as completely distinct from the gentiles around them. As John Mackenzie expresses it 'The haughtiness of the Jew towards the gentile was found sevenfold in the pharisee. Their withdrawal from profane contact meant, in practice, withdrawal from the human race'. (*A New Catholic Commentary on Holy Scripture.*)

In their theology they also laid emphasis upon human freedom as occurring against a background of events ordered by God. Individuals would be held accountable for their use of this freedom. Unlike the sadducees, the pharisees also laid emphasis upon belief in angels and in the general resurrection of the dead. All the theological tenets of pharisaism can be seen as having a positive or negative influence upon Paul's theology. Humanly speaking, it is possible to say that many of the pharisaic beliefs he rejected were those which most conflicted with his instincts as a middle class Roman cosmopolitan. From the perspective of faith it is also possible to see how his encounter with the risen Christ enabled him to reconcile the positive values from both sides of his background.

After his conversion Paul was among the fiercest opponents of any attempt to distinguish between Jewish and gentile converts. To be sons of Abraham now implies a solidarity of faith rather than physical descent or outward religious observance (Rom 4 and Gal 3:29). Indeed the law has now become a symbol of unredemption (Gal 3:13 and Rom 4:13–16). Membership of the new covenant is not based upon observances of the law but upon faith as a response to the quite gratuitous invitation of God in Christ.

Rules about forbidden foods and disputes over holy days (Rom 14; Col 2:16–18); the fact of being circumcised or uncircumcised (1 Cor 7:19, Rom 3:1 and Col 3:11) are all seen as purely secondary to the central question of faith. In the church there is now no essential difference between Jew and gentile (Rom 10:12 and Col 3:11). Divisions between male and female, slave and freed man are seen as equally arbitary, 'for you are all one in Christ Jesus' (Gal 3:28).

But if Paul refused to accept divisions within the christian community he was quite adamant that christians should be 'separated ones' as far as non-christian outsiders were concerned. This essential apartness should be evident from the contrast of life-styles (1 Thes 4:5, 1 Cor 12:2 and Eph 4–5:20). Paul gives a fairly detailed picture of what he regards as the appropriate conduct for a christian. Despite his insistence upon the spirit rather than the letter (Rom 2:29 and 2 Cor 3:6) Paul still has something of the lawyer in his approach. In Paul's letters christian morality sounds much more like a code of conduct than anything we find in the gospels. The moral precepts of the pharisees were popularly regarded as able to hasten the coming of the messiah. In Paul's understanding christian conduct is a direct response to the death and resurrection of Christ, in which the christian is enabled to participate through baptism (Rom 6:5–14 and Col 2:12).

Since Paul is no longer interested in Jewish nationalism he counsels complete collaboration with the secular authorities (Rom 13:1–7). This would fit in well with one side of his personality, but Paul's tendency towards collaboration should not be exaggerated. Christians had not yet experienced Roman persecution and in any case they lived in daily expectation of the second coming of Christ when all political authority would be destroyed (1 Cor 15:24–25).

The most characteristic way in which Paul retains the

pharisaic outlook is in the manner and the extent of his use of the old testament. Apart from the many direct quotes from the old testament Paul makes great use of old testament metaphors and literary types. Frequently he alters the original sense of a quotation by allegorising it or giving it a completely fresh meaning. This behaviour would be considered scandalous in a modern biblical critic but it was quite an acceptable convention in the rabbinic exegesis in which Paul had been educated.

## Signs of Paul's gentile influences

Although Paul was steeped in Jewish culture he was also deeply influenced by his gentile background. How far his theology shows signs of being influenced by gentile religion and Greek philosophy is a matter of debate among scholars. At one time Paul was widely accused of introducing Greek redemption myths and philosophical concepts into christianity, but this view represents a gross over-simplification. Greek thought had been assimilated by judaism well before the beginning of the christian era.

Certainly Paul uses many images which reflect gentile city life. He uses Roman legal terminology (Gal 3:15; 4:1–2; 1 Cor 7:22; Rom 7:1–3 and 7:22) and mercantile expressions (Phm 18; Col 2:14). He also uses images drawn from Greek games; the Corinthian christians are exhorted to emulate the asceticism and dedication of the athlete (1 Cor 9:24–27) and twice Paul pictures himself as a runner in a race (Phil 2:16 and 3:14). Twice in Philippians (1:27 and 3:20) and once in Ephesians (2:19) Paul uses the language of the Greek city state to communicate his understanding of christian citizenship of the people of God. Similarly the description of the church as a body with various members (1 Cor 12:12–27 and Eph 4:25) is very like the political allegory in one of Aesop's fables.

None of what I have been saying is intended to explain away Paul's conversion or to reduce his theology to a conflict between two kinds of social consciousness. Paul's life and thought were a deliberate response to his encounter with the risen Christ on the Damascus road. To understand that response the conflicting cultural background is of vital importance. As Marx said: 'Men make their own history but . . . they do not make it under circumstances chosen by themselves.'

## Christ

The risen Christ whom Paul encountered on the Damascus road was the central reference point for the whole of his subsequent life and thought. Whatever external event may or may not have occurred for Paul, the experience was a direct communication from God to himself (Gal 1:16); an experience on the same level as the resurrection appearances recorded in the gospels (1 Cor 15:8). Paul the Greek would have found the message of a crucified messiah absurd; Saul the pharisee would have found it 'a stumbling block' (1 Cor 1:23). Deut 21:23 teaches that 'a hanged man is accursed by God'. Paul's encounter with Christ enabled him to re-interpret this verse in such a way that the crucified messiah is seen as deliberately taking on the curse of man's sins; deliberately adopting the status of one accursed. In his incarnate state he had become poor so as to enrich mankind (2 Cor 8:9); 'emptied himself', 'taking the form of a servant' (Phil 2:7). By his death he had expressed his ultimate solidarity with man; solidarity with man in accepting the consequences of man's sin. God 'made him to be sin; who knew no sin, so that in him we might become the righteousness of God'. In this perspective Paul was able to see the crucified Christ as the passover lamb sacrificed to mark man's liberation from the power of sin (1 Cor 5:7).

## Paul and the faith of the community

Paul the tentmaker and the former pharisee was able to re-interpret his whole outlook in the light of his conversion, but belief involved entry into a believing community, the church. Despite the very considerable importance he attached to his own personal experience of Christ, however much he may have continued to be influenced by his own background, Paul is the recipient of a living tradition (1 Thes 2:2; 2 Thes 2:15; 3:6; 1 Cor 11:2; 23; 15:1 and 3; Gal 1:9 and 12; Rom 6:17 and Phil 4:9). Frequently he appeals to the practice and belief of the churches and there are many parts of his epistles where he seems to be deliberately quoting from liturgical texts; for example, the doxology in Gal 1:3–5, Rom 11:36 or Phil 4:20; the 'Lord Jesus come' of 1 Cor 16:22 or the hymns found in Phil 2:6–11 and Col 1:15–20.

The epistle to the Ephesians also includes a lot of liturgical material but since scholars are almost equally divided on the question of whether Ephesians was written by Paul or not, we cannot draw any biographical inferences from this epistle.

The really surprising omission in Paul's theology is apparent ignorance of most of the material found in the gospels. It could be said that if Jesus had said or done nothing significant in his life before the last supper (1 Cor 11:23) then Paul's message would have been little different. For Paul the central tradition to be delivered as 'of first importance' is the tradition of Christ's death and resurrection (1 Cor 15:3). There are only seven clear references to sayings of Jesus other than the institution of the eucharist. Only two of these are direct quotations: Rom 12:14 (Mt 5:44 and Lk 6:28) and Rom 13:8 (Mt 22:39–40). 1 Cor 13:2 echoes Mt 17:20 and 17:21 and 1 Cor 9:14 relies on the sayings in Mt 10:10 and Lk 10:7–8. 1 Thes 4:2 and 4:15 refer to unspecified sayings on sexual morality and the general resurrection respectively and 1 Cor 7:10 refers to the sayings on divorce (Mk 10:2–12 and parallels).

To understand this omission it is important to remember that the gospels as we have them were not available at the time Paul was writing. Secondly, and more importantly, it was the risen Christ who had appeared to Paul on the Damascus road and he was much more concerned to stress the saving significance of the risen Christ rather than anything that Jesus may have said or done during his lifetime.

## The kingdom of God

Most surprising of all is the relatively small use of the idea of the kingdom. The phrase 'kingdom of God' (or for Matthew 'kingdom of heaven') occurs more than a hundred times in the synoptic gospels. If we exclude the pastorals, Paul uses the phrase only twelve times. In none of these contexts does the phrase have the central place in his argument. The phrase may not be used much in Paul but the synoptic teaching on the kingdom emerges in other forms. As a future event the kingdom is equated with, and partly replaced by, the second coming of Christ. As a present reality already achieved in Christ the use of the phrase 'kingdom of God' is almost completely abandoned and replaced by the idea of new life in Christ.

Apart from Col 1:13 there is no clear reference to the kingdom as already realised. In four places Paul asserts that the wicked will not 'inherit the kingdom' (1 Cor 6:9; 1 Cor 6:10; Gal. 5:21 and Eph 5:5). In 1 Cor 15:50 it is 'flesh and blood', unredeemed human nature, which will not inherit the kingdom. 2 Thes 1:5, perhaps echoing Mt 5:10 and Lk 6:22, asserts that those who suffer will be 'made worthy of the kingdom of God' and the context makes clear that this is to be expected 'when the Lord Jesus is revealed from heaven' (1:7). In 1 Cor 15:24 Paul speaks of Christ handing over 'the kingdom to God the Father' at the end. Here as in 1 Thes 4:13–17 Paul excludes any allusion to the belief that the messiah would reign with the saints for a thousand years; a belief developed by Jewish apocalyptic writers and taken into the christian tradition in Rev 20:4–6. The absence of this belief in Paul may be attributed to the lack of enthusiasm for apocalyptic in pharisaic theology. In any case, millenarism only becomes widely popular in times of great social distress or persecution.

Only in Colossians (1:13) does Paul clearly refer to the kingdom as a reality already present in history. But Colossians was written towards the end of his life, when his earlier sense of the imminent return of Christ had begun to fade.

## Election and grace

In the synoptics the kingdom of God is seen as entirely gratuitous; repentance is the only qualification; and the kingdom is freely available to social and religious outsiders, but the invitation to the kingdom is always a crisis situation since God's graciousness can also be a judgement on the inadequacy of man's response. In Paul God's

gift of new life in Christ is equally gratuitous. To receive
it men have to turn to God in an act of faith and become
identified with Christ's death through baptism. This gift
is equally available to all, though all must 'appear before
the judgement seat of Christ, so that each one may receive
good or evil according to what he has done in the body'
(2 Cor 5:10).

Paul had too keen a sense of his own unworthiness to
fail to place the initiative in man's salvation firmly with
God. *Righteousness* in Paul's thinking is not man on his
best behaviour, but a power which God communicates
to man through the death and resurrection of Christ
(Phil 3:7–10). Man's redemption is a 'free gift' (Rom
5:15) a making righteous apart from works (Rom 4:6).
Paul's rich sense of the corporate new life in Christ enabled him to perceive man's total moral inadequacy before God; man is 'carnal, sold under sin'. As a christian
who has come alive in Christ, Paul is able to see the corporate deadness of man in his unredeemed state. In
Romans (5:18–19) this state is expressed in terms of
solidarity in sin with Adam; in Colossians it is described
as the 'dominion of darkness', a state of being in bondage
to evil spirits.

Although repentance is implied in Paul's understanding of faith and baptism, he makes only occasional use of
the word. God's kindness is meant to lead man to repentance (Rom 2:4). Man is in a state of ignorance (2 Cor
3:16); characteristically worshipping idols (1 Thes 1:9)
until he 'turns to the Lord'. Man acknowledges that God
has raised Jesus Christ from the dead and this acknow-
ledgement, this act of faith is the guarantee of his salvation
(Rom 10:9). But this is not just an individualistic thing
since Paul frequently equates baptism with the act of

faith and baptism is the initiation into the christian community.

Like the kingdom preached in the gospels this new creation in Christ (Gal 6:15, 2 Cor 5:17) is available to all. Sociologically the early church consisted mostly of poor city dwellers, members of the *lumpen*, and Paul uses this fact to illustrate the gratuitousness of God's invitation. The intellectual sophist (1 Cor 1:20); the powerful and aristocratic (1 Cor 1:26) were not to be found in the early church. 'God chose what is weak in the world to shame the strong' (1 Cor 1:28). In the same way being a Jew provided no special claim on the new life in Christ (Rom 9:6). For Paul God's choice of the redeemed is seen as rooted in his sovereign will alone: 'not because of works but because of his call' (Rom 9:11) and 'not man's will or exertion but upon God's mercy'.

## The Holy Spirit

For Paul the Holy Spirit was the present guarantee of future redemption. To share in the new life in Christ is to participate already in the future kingdom. The presence of the Spirit in the lives of christians was evidence that in a sense at least the new age had already come. Although Paul did not have a developed trinitarian understanding of the identity of the Holy Spirit, he saw the Spirit as playing a vital role in God's communicating of the power of Christ's resurrection to man.

The Spirit is seen as the agent of man's liberation: 'The Lord is the Spirit and where the Spirit is there is freedom' (2 Cor 3:17). The Spirit frees man from slavery to the law (2 Cor 3:6), from 'the desires of the flesh' (unredeemed human nature—Gal 5:16) and from bondage 'to the elemental spirits of the universe' (Gal 4:3). Through the mission of Jesus christians share his status as sons of God. No longer in the relationship of slaves to a master the believers receive the Spirit of Jesus who enables them to address God with the familiar title of *Abba*, 'Father' (Gal 4:6) 'when we cry Abba, Father it is the Spirit himself bearing witness with our spirit that we are children of God' (Rom 8:15–26).

Characteristically the christian community pray through Christ to the Father but the Spirit is seen as the actual source of prayer making up for human weakness, articulating the prayers, and interceding 'for the saints according to the will of God' (Rom 8:26–27). To be 'in the flesh', that is to be in a state of non-freedom, is to be unable to please God and not to be in the Spirit is synonymous with not belonging to Christ (Rom 8:8–9). Those who really do belong to Christ are indwelt by the Spirit of the Father who raised Jesus Christ from the dead. The principle of Christ's resurrection becomes the principle who enables believers to rise from the dead (8:10–11). The gift of the Spirit is seen as the guarantee of the resurrection body; the 'house not made with hands' (2 Cor 5:1–5 cf also 2 Cor 1:22). Being made holy by the Spirit is a primary cause of the salvation of believers (2 Thes 2:13).

The Spirit is the basis of all communication and fellowship between the members of the church. Then, as now, some christians seemed to enjoy ecstatic Spirit possession (1 Cor 12:10–13, 14 and 2 Cor 12:1–7). Miracles and prohecy were also highly regarded and attributed to the Holy Spirit. Paul accepts the value of all these 'gifts of the Spirit' but insists that the Spirit is chiefly exemplified in what unites believers rather than that which differentiates them (1 Cor 12:3, 12–13). The extraordinary gifts of the Spirit have value only in building up the church (1 Cor 14:12). The Spirit is both the channel through

which God's love is received (Rom 5:5) and the currency
through which it is shared.


## The church

This word (Gk *ecclesia*) was probably first used to provide
a name for the local christian congregation which would
distinguish it from the synagogue. In the Septuagint, the
Greek translation of the old testament, the word is used
to translate 'congregation of the Lord' with the additional
sense of a group of people 'called out' to a liturgical
assembly where they could celebrate their covenant relationship with God in solemn worship. The word only
appears twice in the gospels (Mt 16:1 and 18:17).

   In his first two epistles (1 and 2 Thes) Paul uses the
word in the singular to refer to the local christian community (1 Thes 1:1 and 2 Thes 1:1) and in the plural to
refer to 'the churches of God in Christ Jesus which are in
Judaea' (1 Thes 2:14). This use of the word to describe
only the local church continues through Galatians (1:22,
14:15) and in 1 Corinthians (1:2, 4:17, 7:17, 11:16 and
14:33, 16:1 and 16:19), 2 Corinthians (8:1) Romans
(16:1 and 16:16), Philippians and Colossians (4:15 and
16). In 1 Corinthians, however, Paul begins to use the
word in a more developed sense to refer specifically to the
church as a community gathered together for worship;
there are divisions in the liturgical assembly (11:18);
those who abuse the *agape* (fellowship meal) with gluttony 'despise the church of God' (11:22); Paul prefers
the worshippers to comprehend the words used 'in
church' (14:19, 23); where there is no interpreter of
tongues the people with the gift of tongues should 'keep
silence in church' (14:28); similarly women should 'keep
silence in church' (14:34–35). Paul also uses the word to

refer to the church in a more universal sense: 'I persecuted the church of God' (1 Cor 15:9; cf Gal 1:13 and
Phil 3:6). In 1 Cor 12:28 Paul refers to the various
ministries in the church and clearly refers to the universal
church ('St Paul cannot be saying that God has set
Apostles in the local congregation', Richardson *An Introduction to the New Testament* London, 1938).

The unity of the church is founded upon Christ (1 Cor
12:8) and expressed sacramentally through baptism. In
another sense christians are seen as one body through
sharing in the one eucharistic bread and cup (1 Cor 10:
16–18). By consumption of the body of Christ christians
become his body. In chapter 12 Paul is using the Greek
metaphor of the citizens of a state being like different
members of the human body; each having a different function but each working with the rest for the good of the
whole. It is the light of this understanding of what it
means to belong to the church that Paul inveighs against
a christian, who is part of Christ's body, becoming one
flesh with a prostitute (1 Cor 6:15).

Later, in Col 1:18 and 24, Paul specifically identifies
the body of Christ as the church. But the metaphor has
changed a little: Christ is now seen as the head of the
body. This image is explained and extended in Eph 4:16.
Christ is the head of the church in the sense that each
member is dependent upon and obliged to obey the head.
Paul suggests that the woman is subordinate to man as
the head in the marriage relationship; 'the head of a
woman is her husband' 1 Cor 11:3. This enables the
writer of Ephesians to switch the image from head-body
relationship to man-woman relationship. The church,
like the woman, is subordinate to her husband and like
the woman she is one body with him (Eph 5:21–33).

Other images of the church are also employed. Paul

refers to the church as 'the Jerusalem above' (Gal 4:26) as a household (Gal 6:10); as 'the Israel of God' (Gal 6:16); as a field (1 Cor 3:9) and as 'the temple of the living God' (2 Cor 6:16). This image of the church as a building recurs in 1 Thes 5:11 ('build one another up'), 1 Cor 3:9 ('you are God's field, God's building'); 1 Cor 10:23 ('not all things build up'); 1 Cor 14:12 refers to 'building up the church' through the gifts of prophecy. In Gal 2:9 he refers to Peter and John as being thought of as 'pillars' and in 2 Cor 6:16 says 'we are the temple of the living God'. In three places in 2 Corinthians Paul sees his ministry as one of building up the Corinthian church (10:8, 12:19 and 13:10) and the same image is employed in Rom 15:20 and Col 2:7. As with the image of the body Ephesians offers the most detailed elaboration of the metaphor (see Eph 2:19–22 and 4:12–16 which combines the two metaphors and talks about 'the whole body upbuilding itself in love'). Like the early christians the Qumran community had thought of themselves as the temple and in both cases the word conveyed the idea of a messianic community enshrining the presence of God.

## The organization of the church

Paul does not give us much information about the practical organisation of the churches to which he is writing. In 1 Corinthians in particular he gives us a vivid picture of the spontaneous character of the church meetings: characterised by the *agape* or fellowship meal, the eucharist itself and ecstatic prophecyings and speaking in tongues, but he answers none of the kind of questions which our modern ecumenists might ask: who celebrated the eucharist? what relationship did the different ministries have with the authority of the apostle? were babies ever baptised?

In 1 Cor 12 Paul refers to a number of ministries (Gk *diakonoi*): apostles, prophets, teachers, workers of miracles, healers, helpers, administrators and speakers in tongues. It is obvious that all these ministries were not ministries at all in the modern clerical sense. Verses 12–13 of the same chapter seems to be arguing that all christians are ministers. Many of the specific ministers are 'gifts' of the Spirit discoverable in different individuals in the church.

The term 'apostle' seems to cover two categories of people: the apostles of the Lord, among whom Paul numbered himself, and the apostles of the churches.

Only the twelve, Paul himself and 'James the Lord's brother' (Gal 1:19) belong to the first category. James may have been included out of respect or in view of his having been the recipient of a resurrection appearance by Christ (1 Cor 15:9). Part of Paul's own claim to be an apostle seems to have rested upon his encounter with the risen Christ but it cannot have rested upon this alone since he tells us of a further five hundred who had the same privilege (1 Cor 15:6). The authority of an apostle derives from a direct commission from the Lord himself.

The word 'apostle' (literally 'one sent') was originally used of a leader in a naval expedition, but it seems likely that it may have come into use among christians as the Greek equivalent of the Hebrew *shaliach* or fully accredited representative and plenipotentiary. The 'apostles of the churches', on the other hand, may mean simply the messengers of the churches.

These 'messengers of the churches' (2 Cor 8:23) seem to have included little known persons like Andronicus and Junius, possibly a woman, who was a relation of Paul's (Rom 16:7). This verse could indicate simply that Andronicus and Junias were well known to the apostles, but this is not a very widely held view. Epaphroditus is referred to as an *apostolos* in Phil 2:25. Whether these 'messengers' became the separate order of 'apostles' referred to in the *Didache* remains an open question.

Unless Paul wrote the pastoral epistles, which is unlikely, we have no definite grounds for supposing that Paul knew of any 'ordained ministry' in the modern sense. The 'bishops' and 'deacons' at Philippi might have been examples of the emergent church order evident later in the pastorals but there is no mention of 'bishops' (*episcopoi*) in the lists of the church ministries in 1 Cor 12 and Rom 12:6–18. In the Corinthian list it has been suggested that the 'administrators' (1 Cor 12:28) may have been the bishops and the 'helpers' the deacons, but there is no reason to suppose so. What seems most likely is that the churches were loosely constituted, rather informal communities with flexible forms of ministry. Their relationship with each other would have been through their appointed 'messengers' and the overall discipline would have been exercised by whatever apostle could claim to be the founding father of the community. The apostles' own authority and commission was derived directly from the risen Lord.

Unfortunately Paul does not tell us much of his relationship with the other apostles. Galatians makes clear that he had a bitter controversy with the Jerusalem leadership of Peter and James but the fact that he went to Jerusalem at all indicates a concern for unity on the important question of the status of gentile converts in the church.

### The second coming

The image of the church as the temple, Jerusalem or the new Israel has to be understood against the background of Paul's view of history. For Paul human history falls into three distinct chapters; the period before the law which lasted from Adam to Moses (Rom 5:14); the period of the law which lasted until the time of Christ; and finally the period between Christ's first coming and second coming. In the gospels the kingdom is sometimes referred to as already established with the coming of Christ and sometimes seen as still to come. This ambiguity is carried over in Paul.

As a former pharisee Paul lays great emphasis upon the resurrection of the body. Christ will come again (1 Thes 4:15, 2 Thes 1:10 and 2:13) and the dead will rise with bodies (1 Thes 4:17 and 1 Cor 4:5). This will be followed by the judgement (2 Cor 5:10) and the glorification of the elect (1 Thes 4:16). 1 and 2 Thessalonians, the earliest epistles, are completely dominated by the daily expectation of these events. Paul looks forward to boasting of the Thessalonians at the coming of Christ (2:19) and prays that they may be ready for this event (3:13 and 5:23). Like the kingdom Christ's return will be as unexpected as a burglary (1 Thes 5:5, compare Lk 12:39). He even seems to expect that some of them will be still alive at the second coming. The relationship between this future hope and the sacramental life of the christian now is not yet clear (1 Thes 4:15).

With the passage of time Paul's understanding on this topic changed considerably. In 2 Cor 5:1–10 and Phil 1:23 Paul considers the possibility of some christians dying before Christ comes again. From thinking of man's redemption as primarily in the future, Paul develops a tension between the judgement and glory which are already a reality and their fulfilment which comes at the

end time. The christians 'have the first fruits of the Spirit'
but they still join with the whole created order in long-
ing 'for adoption as sons, the redemption of our bodies'
(Rom 8:23). In the captivity epistles the emphasis moves
more and more towards the new life as already enjoyed.
Christians are already citizens of heaven (Phil 3:20) who
have been raised in baptism (Col 2:12) and are somehow
already exalted 'in the heavenly places in Christ Jesus'
(Eph 2:6).

## Paul and subsequent theology

Paul was the first, and one of the greatest, if not indeed
*the* greatest christian theologian. Calvinists, lutherans
and counter-reformation catholics have all claimed St
Paul as their own. It was St Augustine of Hippo who
developed some of Paul's insights on grace, free will, election and original sin in the course of his controversy with
the British monk Pelagius, who asserted a doctrine of
free will which undermined the other three Pauline
doctrines. Augustine's interpretation of Paul's teaching
on grace is also central to the controversy over quietism
and Jansenism in the seventeenth century.

Nineteenth-century liberal protestantism tended to
regard Paul as the man who had turned the simple ethical
creed of the 'fatherhood of God and the brotherhood of
man' into a Greek salvation myth with sacraments and a
divine redeemer. Some modern scholars still regard Paul
as the importer of alien influences into christianity. The
extent to which this is true and the point at which it becomes dangerous are both points of contention however.
Paul's chief genius lay in the way in which he adapted
Jewish theology to a gentile audience, but he still re-

mained very much in the Jewish tradition and very much in the same tradition as the most primitive material in the synoptic gospels.

## The importance of Paul for today

As with all historical religions christianity has the problem of translating its gospel out of categories of thought which have lost their relevance and expressing them in new ways. Understood properly Paul can help us in this task.

As I have tried to show Paul shared the limitations of tentmaker with the limitations of a pharisee. He tolerated the institution of slavery and warmly supported the subordinate role of women in contemporary society. On a variety of subjects from homosexuality to old testament exegis, he was completely a child of his time. In whatever sense we understand Paul's epistles as the word of God, we cannot mean that the christian must be simply culturally regressive. Paul's great theological genius lay in rejecting exactly this tendency.

Paul's faith centred so strongly upon the person of the risen Christ that he had a very firm grasp of essentials. When more conservative christians tried to limit christianity to its original Jewish perspectives, Paul was able to insist upon the centrality of Christ through whom God bestows salvation as a free gift. To understand the gratuitousness of salvation in this way was to realise, in the words of Karl Rahner, 'that every human being is to become a christian from the point at which he himself is placed'. ('Paul Apostle for Today', *Mission and Grace* vol iii, p. 19.)

The church of today has witnessed the final collapse of christendom and the result of the attempt to fuse the christian and secular order into one christian civilisation.

For many christians the secularisation of our society is viewed with dismay. They can learn from Paul that the mystery of God's election transcends cultural frontiers. Christ is no more limited to christendom that he was to judaism. Like Paul the apostolic christian must 'become all things to all men' (1 Cor 9:22) consistently refusing to restrict Christ to his own cultural insights.

Another aspect of the contemporary situation is the widespread dissatisfaction with institutional religion and within Roman catholicism at least a degeneration into factionalism. Against these tendencies Paul's vision of the church is of a transcendent reality. In the last analysis personalities are unimportant (see 1 Cor 1:12–13), even articulate theologians and impressive preachers are not to be expected. The importance of the christian community lies not in what it is but in what it is called to be. Paul constantly returns to the theme of christian unity and brotherly love within the christian community and yet he finds this perfectly consistent with diversities of ministries and with frank and open criticism of the Jerusalem leadership of Peter and James (Gal 2).

In doctrine Paul repeatedly lays stress upon the importance of the tradition he has received and yet his theology is subject to a steady process of development; Colossians, written towards the end of his life, is a case in point. Seeking to counter the Colossian heresy he takes over some of its main ideas, alters their meaning and incorporates them into his theology of Christ as the cosmic redeemer.

Paul is a model for both the theologian and the missionary and the study of his epistles offers many insights for the church's understanding of its role in the world. Above all, however, Paul offers as the testimony of an unshakable sense of what is really important: 'whatever gain I had, I counted as loss for the sake of Christ . . . for his sake I have suffered the loss of all things and count them as refuse, in order that I may gain Christ' (Phil 3:7–8).

# Life and writings of St Paul

Conversion of Paul (Ac 9:1–19)
departs to Arabia (Gal 1:17)
3 years later returns to Damascus (2 Cor 11:32 and Ac 9:23–25)
Visit to Jerusalem and journey to Caesarea, Syria and Cilicia (Ac 9:30 and Gal 1:21–24)
Helps Barnabas in evangelisation of Antioch (Ac 11:25)
44 AD Paul and Barnabas take boat to Jerusalem during famine (Ac 11:25 and ?Gal 2:1–10)

*First missionary journey* (Ac 12:25–15)
Council of Jerusalem (Gal 2:6–9, Ac 15)
50 AD or 57 AD (North Galatian theory) GALATIANS

*Second missionary journey* (Ac 16–18:28)
At conclusion of this missionary journey Paul spends eighteen months at Corinth 51/52 AD (proconsulship of Gallio, Ac 18:42)
During this time he writes:
1 and 2 THESSALONIANS

*Third missionary journey* (Ac 19–20:17)
Paul spends two years at Ephesus at school of Tyranus
1 CORINTHIANS (57 AD)
Flees to Macedonia where he writes:
GALATIANS (or 50 AD on the South Galatian theory)
2 CORINTHIANS

Spends three months at Achaia
ROMANS
Paul in Jerusalem (Ac 21–26:32) and Caesarea

*Last journey* (Ac 27:1–28:31)

Paul in Rome 61–63 AD
Writes 'captivity epistles':
PHILIPPIANS
COLOSSIANS
(EPHESIANS)
PHILEMON

# Book list

Amiot *Key Concepts in Paul*, New York 1962

Cerfaux *Christ in the Theology of St Paul*, New York 1959

Cullmann *The Christian in the Theology of St Paul*, New York 1959

Dodd *The Meaning of Paul for Today*, paperback ed London 1958

Fitzmyer 'Pauline Theology' in the *Jerome Biblical Commentary*, London 1968. (This essay, a classic of its kind, was also published as a separate volume. Prentice-Hall, NJ)

Hunter *Paul and his Predecessors*, revised ed London 1961

# 1 and 2 Thessalonians

*Mervyn Davies*

# Introduction

# The Thessalonian letters

Paul's letters to the church at Thessalonica contain mostly practical comments on the situation in this early christian community. Apart from some interesting insights into the way of life of the early church and some controversial remarks on morality, perhaps their chief interest lies in what they have to say about eschatology and the christian life.

Christians have always believed that Christ will come again and that when he does, this order of things will cease. From the beginning there was debate not only as to when this would happen but also about what this doctrine meant. This problem was further complicated by the fact that the doctrine underwent successive 'revisions'. At first, christians seem to have believed that the second coming of Christ was imminent, with the result that the christian life was interpreted very much in terms of waiting for this to happen rather than of a positive moral life. Paul has some trenchant things to say about this in these letters. But as time went on, the early church began to see things rather differently, believing that although Christ would come soon, it would only be when the work of the Spirit was done. More thought was given to the function of the church, ideas about the person and work of Christ developed and so did teaching about the life of the christian in the world.

Much of this development was undoubtedly due to the missionary activity of the church and especially of Paul amongst the gentiles, because this not only brought the preachers of the gospel into contact with different ideas, but the problems endemic in setting up christian communities forced the church to consider further the implications of its message. Instead of thinking of Christ as wholly absent, christians began to realise that he was mysteriously present, even though he would come again. The cross, far from being a disaster, was seen in the light of the resurrection to be the pivotal point of the new hope.

Paul's letters to the Thessalonians (probably one of the earliest of the new testament writings which have survived) should be seen as situated within this conversation that was going on amongst the early thinkers in the church, and there seems to be general agreement amongst scholars that his views underwent some change during the years he was writing (although how much is a matter of dispute). From his letters we can see that Paul was very much concerned with the relationship of Christ to his followers, not only in the present, but in the future when Christ would come again. What we have here is perhaps his earliest extant views on the matter and these should be compared with some of his later writings.

But this is also a contemporary problem, because the christian believes that man has a future both within and beyond this temporal existence, but in what this consists and how we are to prepare for it is the theological problem which is raised for us by these letters. What do we mean by heaven, hell and the afterlife and what help can we get from contemporary writings to understand these things? Can one be a christian and *not* believe in an afterlife?

These two letters were written to the christian community in Thessalonica, which was one of the three cities in Macedonia which Paul chose to visit on his second missionary journey, accompanied by Silvanus (otherwise known as Silas) and Timothy. It was a large port (its modern name is Salonika), on the north-east coast of Greece and situated on the Via Egnatia, the imperial highway across Greece to Asia Minor. Not only was it the capital city of Macedonia, it was also a free city in the Roman empire, with its own system of government. As in many of the larger towns of the empire, there was a flourishing Jewish community with a synagogue (Ac 17:1) which may well have made some converts from paganism. Paul and his companions came to Thessalonica from Philippi in the north where he and Silvanus had been imprisoned. At first they seem to have had considerable success amongst both the Jewish and the Greek population (Ac 17:4). In the first letter (1:9) Paul suggests that quite a lot of his converts may have been pagans, but it is not certain whether they were ex-pagans who had become Jews, or whether they were pagans who had become christian, finding the rather nationalistic religion of judaism unattractive. Whatever the situation, Paul's success led to violent action on the part of those Jews who had rejected his teaching. They stirred up the mob and attacked Jason's house in which Paul and his companions were staying. Neither Paul nor the others were there at the time, but Jason and some fellow christians were dragged before the magistrates on the charge of acknowledging another king besides Caesar. Jason was 'bound over' to keep the peace and Paul and Silvanus were sent away from the city to Berea. But the trouble-makers followed

after him from Thessalonica and he was forced to make
for Athens. There Paul sent Timothy to Thessalonica to
find out how the new christian community was faring before moving on to Corinth. The first letter was written on
Timothy's return.

This information, which is recorded in Acts, enables
us to date the Thessalonian letters with some accuracy, for
while Paul was in Corinth the Jews made another attack
on him and had him brought before Gallio, the pro-
consul of Achaia (Ac 18:12). But Gallio, seeing that the
dispute was merely a matter of theology, drove him and
his accusers out, telling them to settle their disputes
among themselves. We know from an inscription at
Delphi that Gallio became pro-consul after the 26th
proclamation of Claudius as emperor, sometime between
August 51 and August 52. If Paul appeared before Gallio
shortly after he assumed office (this usually happened in
midsummer) and towards the end of Paul's eighteen-
month stay in the city, it seems likely that the first letter
to the Thessalonians was written just after Paul's arrival
in Corinth and that the second letter was written not long
afterwards, in the early part of 51 AD, although some
scholars date them a year earlier than this.

Assuming that both these letters are by Paul (and there
seems to be no really convincing reason to doubt this),
what was Paul trying to achieve in writing to the Thessalonians?

The first letter was clearly written as a reaction to what
Timothy had reported of the Thessalonian situation since
their departure. Paul congratulates the Thessalonians for
the way in which they have received the word of God and
remained faithful to it despite considerable hostility. He
then refutes slanderous reports that have been made
about him by his Jewish opponents and encourages the

church to have courage to endure the persecution they are receiving from their fellow-countrymen. In the last two chapters of the letter, Paul shows how he thinks christian morality must differ from that of paganism and then tries to correct a misunderstanding about the second coming of Christ.

The second letter is shorter and gives proportionately more space to the problem of eschatology. Perhaps the Thessalonians had not understood what he was saying in his first letter, but Paul also seems to suggest that he had heard that another letter, purporting to be from him, and containing false eschatological teaching, had been circulating in the Thessalonian church. The letter seems to have suggested that the day of the Lord had already come and that the Anti-Christ was abroad. It may, in fact, have put forward similar views to those canvassed by some religious sects today who try to give a date and time for the 'end of the world'. Adventism seems to have been a problem for the early church from the start and so Paul is very anxious to correct this false teaching and sets out the signs by which believers may know that the coming of Christ is imminent. The problem facing contemporary students of the bible is just how we should interpret this teaching, which bears considerable resemblance to Mk 13. These ideas were steeped in the old testament and they have to be interpreted with the old testament message in mind, for when early christian thinkers began to reflect on the prophecies of the messiah and the golden age that was to come, they found ready categories in which to understand the Christ-event. They saw that the scriptures had been fulfilled in and by Christ and so much of the old testament message and hope was re-interpreted christologically. As a part of this process, it was natural that beliefs connected with the day of the Lord in the old testament, the day on which Yahweh would reveal his final judgement on the world and its nations and Israel would be delivered by the hand of God, should be transferred to Christ himself as *the* revelation of God. The faith of Israel was that history had a purpose given by God and that man was an integral part of this. This purpose would be fully revealed and fully realised in the new age which christians believed had already come in Christ. The proof of this was Christ's resurrection, the giving of the Spirit and the miraculous growth of the early church. But they could see that there was much left to be done. The old order was taking a long time to pass away, the radical transformation of mankind had not yet occurred—or at least, not in its fulness. And so the early christians, with the aid of old testament concepts derived from apocalyptic writing, began to look forward to a final consummation, a completion of the definitive work begun by Christ. The scriptures could only be completed by the final rout of evil which would occur when Christ revealed himself again.

The theological problem with which we, too, are concerned is that though something definitive did happen in Christ, a decisive move was made against evil, nevertheless evil is still with us. We live in a world of injustice, hatred, famine and war. The task of transforming the world is very much ours but, we ask, is there going to be a fulfilment and if so what will it be? It is this problem that we have to consider, with the help of these letters.

## Book list

1. *The Jerusalem Bible*. The notes and introduction to the Pauline epistles make a useful short guide.
2. *Thessalonians*, Moffat NT commentary, by W. Neil. A very comprehensive study.

3. *Peake's Commentary*, 1 and 2 Thessalonians, is a much shorter version of W. Neil's Moffat commentary. Clear and easy to consult.

4. *Letters of Paul to the Philippians and the Thessalonians*, Cambridge Bible Commentary, by Kenneth Grayston. Very readable indeed.

5. *New Testament Introduction: The Pauline Epistles*, Donald Guthrie. Contains all the technical information that might be needed.

6. *The Apostolic Preaching and its Developments*, C. H. Dodd. An invaluable short study for anyone who wants to delve further.

7. *Jesus and his coming*, J. A. T. Robinson. This has an important and interesting section on Thessalonians.

8. Karl Rahner's *Theology of Death* is good ancillary reading.

# 1

# Thanksgiving for the faith of the church at Thessalonica
# 1 Thes 1:1–10

After the greeting at the head of this letter comes a prayer of thanks to God for the outstanding christian life of the newly-founded Thessalonian church. From his other letters, as well as this one, we get a strong impression that Paul always tried to keep in close touch with the churches he had founded, encouraging, teaching and correcting them personally, through letters and personal representatives (cf 2 Cor 9:28). He was in no sense a remote pastor but one who intimately shared the joys and sufferings of his communities.

The reason for his evident joy here is the success of the Thessalonian mission, evidenced by the 'active faith and labour of love and patient hope in our Lord Jesus Christ' of the congregation. These words remind us of the great hymn of love (1 Cor 13) in which Paul summarises the essential nature of a christian. This theme of faith, love and hope occurs so often in his writings that it is thought that it may have been part of the church's pre-pauline tradition of what it meant to be a christian. Other instances of it occur at Col 1:4–5; Gal 5:5–6; Rom 5:2–5; 1 Pet 1:1–2. The order here is interesting: faith, love, hope: it may, in Paul's mind, provide a convenient frame-

work for what he is going to say in both his letters, namely
that the well-spring of the christian life is faith in Christ
and in what he has done for us. This faith is in turn expressed in the love of the christian for God and his fellow-
men (and not in idleness or selfishness, as Paul remarks in
the second letter). But both this faith and love look forward to a completion in the future when Christ will come
again. The christian lives both fully in the present, fighting against evil and trying to live a life of love, but also he
looks forward to the completion of Christ's work at some
future time. Both letters stress this and Paul spells it out
for them here by reminding the Thessalonians that they
received the gospel in 'full conviction' (1:5), becoming
'imitators of us and of the Lord' so that 'you became an
example' (1:6–7) and now 'wait for his (God's) Son from
heaven' (1:10).

It is important to see how, for Paul, faith, love, hope
are not three distinct things in the sense that it is really
possible to have one without the others (it was just this
point that was the basis of some of Luther's disputes with
catholic theologians). You cannot be a christian, on Paul's
view, unless all three are present: true faith *must* show
itself in action and look forward in hope. Love must be
based on a personal relationship with Christ and long for
the fulfilment of God's purpose for the world which
Christ has promised to bring. Hope in the future is based
on what Christ has already done for us by the cross and
resurrection and on a desire to bring Christ into the
present by a life of love. There are many senses of the
word 'faith' in Paul's writings, but underlying them all is
the idea of faith as a personal relationship of trust in
Christ as our Lord and brother. It is not intellectual
assent to a corpus of statements that Paul regards as the
paradigm of faith, but something alive, analogous to the

way in which a man has trust in a close friend or a wife. This must show itself in love and hope for the future, or it is nothing. Yet Paul is not being anti-intellectual; he is saying that all faith is exploratory in the way that personal relationships are. It is in this way that we become God's sons (Col 3:26–4:7).

Paul does not have in mind here the dispute about faith and the law which concerned him in the letter to the Galatians. He believed, as did the other writers of the new testament, that to have a relationship with Christ which is not one of love (both for him and our fellowmen) is to have a relationship which is dead, no relationship at all. The sign that this relationship is alive is this 'labour of love and steadfastness of hope in our Lord Jesus Christ' of which he speaks here.

But Paul also reminds us that what distinguishes the christian from the pagan is this hope for the future. This is not an anaesthetic by which we escape from the harsh realities of the present, as Marx thought, but a basis for life in that we realise we have a fundamental part to play in the realisation of that future. Paul and his fellow-christians looked forward to a time when Christ would come again and God's purpose for the world would be revealed and completed. This was not a hope with dubious prospects of fulfilment, because Christ's promises are assured by the resurrection. It is on this that our faith is grounded. It was not a belief to make the christian sit back and wait for the end (some did think this and Paul attacks them vigorously in these letters) but, on the contrary, to make them work all the harder to build up the community of love in preparation for what was to come. It must have been for this that Paul praised the Thessalonian church.

Paul tells us that the Thessalonians had turned from

idols 'to serve a living and true God' (1 : 9) and seems to
suggest that the majority of his converts had been not
Jews but followers of the Greek religion. Idol worship
was regarded as abhorrent by both Jews and christians
alike. It was a debased and corrupt form of religion because no one can ever see the face of God (Deut 4 : 15)
and so the worship of idols could only be regarded as a
sham and a cheat, not just obscuring the truth but
actively leading men away from it (*eidolon*, the Greek
word, originally meant 'phantom' or something belonging
to the imagination). Converting such men to christianity
was thus no mean achievement and Paul is justifiably
proud of them and the fact that they have persevered in
the new faith. They have, in John's language, truly passed
from darkness to light.

   *1. How should the church be showing its life of faith,
love and hope amongst today's problems?*
   *2. Are there any equivalents today to the pagan idols of
the past from which men must be converted?*

# 2

# The conduct of an apostle
# 1 Thes 2:1–12

When Paul claims that his visit to the Thessalonians was 'not in vain', he is referring to the fact, mentioned in the previous chapter, that he brought the gospel 'in power and the Holy Spirit'. It was this that gave it authenticity and ensured his success, because the gospel comes not from men but from God and its reception by men depends on Christ and the Holy Spirit. But he brought the gospel, he reminds them, in the teeth of opposition and at the cost of great personal suffering (Ac 16:12). He refers in passing to the incidents at Philippi (2:2) where he cured a slave girl, possessed by some spirit, who made money for her masters by divination. His curing of her meant that her owners lost their source of trade and a riot developed in which even the magistrates joined the crowd in tearing their clothes from their backs and beating them with rods (Ac 16:19–24). Despite this treatment, Paul and his companions escaped from prison and came to Thessalonica to spread the gospel. Again they encountered great opposition, especially from the Jews who lived there. Paul points out here and elsewhere in the two letters that the kind of commitment made by a christian demands from him the willingness to suffer for Christ's sake. In this he was but echoing the teaching of Christ who constantly pointed out to his followers that to be a disciple meant being prepared to leave everything for his sake and to take the consequences of rejection, suffering and possibly death (Mk 8:34–5; Mt 10:38; Lk 17:33). Indeed T. W. Manson has pointed out that these conditions of discipleship are practically identical with the conditions laid down by Jesus for entry into the kingdom, so that for those prepared to give themselves to Christ in faith, the kingdom has already come in some sense. The true apostle expects this kind of treatment and accepts it from God 'who tests our hearts'.

The next few verses (2:5–12) seem to suggest that a number of charges were made against him by his Jewish opponents which he is here refuting. Perhaps there had been a well-mounted smear-campaign against him by the Jews, accusing him of being concerned with personal gain and possibly even of sexual immorality (2:3). The imputation seems to have been also that he was a kind of trickster (2:3) whereas he asserts that he toiled night and day to preach the gospel and that he supported himself by his own trade (2:9). Paul has occasion to mention this again in the second letter, which perhaps indicates how sensitive he was to this kind of attack. He had been gentle and affectionate towards them, not from any ulterior motives, but because he had become genuinely fond of them. His opponents were obviously prepared to make capital out of anything that could be dubiously construed. In Ac 18:4 Paul is described as a tent-maker or leather-worker and it is clear from the references in these letters and in other places that this was how he supported himself so that he might be free to preach the word of God.

*1. What should be a christian's reaction to unjust acts done to him?*

2. *Is Paul's principle of being self-supporting practicable for the clergy today?*

# 3

# The lot of a christian
# 1 Thes 2:13–3:13

**1 Thes 2:13–20. Testing christian understanding**

In this section Paul says much more about suffering and
its value as part of the christian life. But first of all, he
praises the Thessalonians for accepting the gospel not as
'the word of men, but as it really is, the word of God'.
This is really a development of his theme of faith begun
in the first chapter. Paul is attributing to the Thessalonians the power of discernment that is a result of faith.
They can distinguish the true from the false, the word of
God from the word of men. But how? This was a problem
that worried the prophets in the old testament. How
could they demonstrate that the word of the false prophets
did not come from Yahweh but was fundamentally
opposed to his will? Jeremiah searched for practical
criteria by which they could be distinguished and condemned (Jer 23; cf also 1 Kg 22:11ff; Mic 3:5; Deut
18:21). No really satisfactory criteria emerged except that
ultimately the message of the prophet who had a genuine
insight into the mysterious work of God remained,
whereas the other was rejected. Jesus' rejection of much
of the understanding of his contemporaries was based on
the fact that he had a true insight into the purpose of
God, whereas theirs had been lost or distorted.

This problem of discernment has always been with the

43

church. While agreeing that something definitive has been given in Christ, this process of understanding must go on in the church. 'Faith seeks understanding' as St Anselm was to say many centuries later at the beginning of the *Proslogion*. The church seeks understanding under the guidance of the Spirit, an activity which belongs to every member of the church, as the Vatican council teaches us. But on what grounds is one belief rejected and another retained? How are we to know what is a genuine explicitation of revelation from what is spurious? Paul seems to suggest here that this is something to do with faith, referring things back to Christ, testing them against our relationship with him, just as one might test a report of somebody's behaviour against one's experience of him. The power of discernment belongs to the Thessalonians, who imitated the christianity of Judea, just as it must be a part of any contemporary christian life.

The christian must suffer. Paul is adamant about this and he develops here what later came to be called a theology of the 'imitation of Christ'. Just as Christ suffered at the hands of his own people, so did the early christians in Judea, and so did they, the Thessalonians, at the hands of their fellow-citizens. They must expect it.

*1. Bearing in mind some of the controversies of recent years, how is the truth of the gospel to be explored by the church today?*

*2. How should we talk about the 'authority of the church' in the interpretation of scripture?*

*3. Has the church overemphasised suffering in the past? Is it possible to have a positive attitude towards it?*

## 1 Thes 2:17–3:13. The power of evil and the return of Christ

Paul narrates in this section what had happened to him and his companions since his visit to Thessalonica (Ac 17:10ff) but there are certain phrases which suggest that Paul has the persecution of christians very much to the forefront of his mind, especially when he says 'you yourselves know that this is to be our lot'. This opposition comes not just from men, however, but from Satan who, he says, prevented his return to Thessalonica.

Satan is rarely mentioned in the old testament, partly because there was a tendency in old testament theology to attribute both good and evil to the will of God and not to speculate further. How the idea of the devil or Satan developed is not at all certain, but it must have been partly due to dualistic influences and partly to a sense of the inappropriateness of making God responsible for evil in any but a permissive sense. Some mention is made of him in Zech 3:1, Job 1:6 and 1 Chron 21:1, in which he is gradually seen as an independent being able to act contrary to God's will. In the gospels we find mention made of two kingdoms which are ruled over by God and Satan respectively, and in the parable of the sower Christ explains that it is Satan who comes and takes away the seed of faith (Mk 4:15). Christ also teaches that it is Satan who is the source of temptation, the provoker of human wickedness (Mk 1:13; 8:33 and Lk 13:6). Christ comes directly in conflict with Satan by his miracles of healing, his cross and his resurrection. In Paul's view, therefore, the christian is a son of God by his faith but he is also the prey of the devil. Evil is thus not just what men do, but a force, a kingdom of darkness which can destroy a man. In his other letters, Paul sees this force of evil as having cosmic dimensions. There are principalities, powers and

elements all belonging to the force of evil which holds
sway in the world but whose grip must ultimately be
destroyed. This is the reason why a christian must suffer:
battle is joined against evil as a result of the coming of
Christ. Christ has conquered sin and death, but the effects
of his victory must be made actual by the church under
the Spirit through the course of history. No new testament writer was tempted to underestimate the insidious
power of evil which saps at the sources of good within a
man until it destroys him.

In 2:19 Paul speaks of the Thessalonians as his 'hope
or joy or crown of boasting before our Lord Jesus at his
coming'. This is the first of several occasions in Paul's
letters where he uses the Greek word *parousia* in speaking
of the expected arrival of Christ. From the casual way in
which it is mentioned, we can reasonably be sure that the
Thessalonians were familiar with the word. It is used here
in the technical sense of the return of the glorified Christ
to earth (cf 1 Thes 3:13; 4:15; 5:23 and 2 Thes 1:8) and
has the added significance of Christ coming again with
messianic power (cf Jas 5:7; 2 Pet 1:16). Only then will
Christ be fully manifested to his people. A threefold picture is thus emerging of the christian: by his faith, he can
discern the true word from the false, through his faith he
will suffer and because of it he will see the *parousia*.

The early christians had felt the absence of Christ very
acutely at first and the first chapter of Acts gives us something of the picture of gloom that must have followed
Christ's departure from their company. But gradually, as
the church evolved its own distinctive kind of worship
and differentiated itself from judaism, they began to
realise the extent of Christ's mysterious presence within
the church, especially in the sacraments. They believed
that Christ was to be encountered in the christian com-

munity (1 Cor 10:15) but even so they looked forward to
a time when they would see Christ 'face to face' and when
every rule and kingdom hostile to God would be
destroyed (1 Cor 15:24). This will happen when faith,
the church, and this mode of existence have, like Marx's
state, 'withered away'. Christ is therefore present to men
in two ways: sacramentally in the church, and fully revealed in heaven. This preoccupation of the early church
with the *parousia* came about because early christians
could see that the work of Christ had not reached its
climax. He must come again to finish what he began and
call all things back to God. Paul seems to slightly change
his view in later letters where he speaks of this universal
reconciliation having already taken place on the cross
(Col 1:13–22). By and large, as time went on, the second
coming of Christ was emphasised less as realisation grew
of how Christ through the Spirit is still with the church.
Here Paul is emphatic that Christ will come soon, and
that therefore the christian is characterised by being a
man of love and holiness, waiting for this to happen.

   *1. Is 'Satan' still a useful term to use when discussing
evil?*
   *2. How should we interpret Paul's view that the chris-
tian life is one lived in expectation of the* parousia?

# 4

## The christian way of life
## 1 Thes 4:1–12

Quite why Paul should have raised the question of sexual morality at this stage is not altogether clear. The general laudatory tone of the letter would not lead the reader to suppose that immorality of this kind was rife among the Thessalonian christians, although it is possible that some of them may have found it difficult to live the christian ethic having been recent converts from paganism. R. H. Lightfoot suggested that there may have been a mystery religion cult indulging in sexual orgies in Thessalonica which may have had considerable influence, so that Paul felt he had to issue a stern warning. But this is conjecture and there may well be other explanations, not least that this was something that Paul felt very strongly about anyway (cf the Corinthian letters) and that experiences in other cities may have led him to issue warnings to the other communities he had founded.

Paul stresses at the beginning that although they learnt from him 'how to live and to please God' this is also an ongoing process by which men become holy. Put another way, we might say that the christian life is a process of becoming what we are; fully human and developed in all our faculties. The instructions of which Paul speaks were the preaching and the teaching of the early church based upon the gospel of Christ himself. Indeed, Paul regarded

himself as sent to give the gospel to the gentiles, the
gospel of Christ, the most human of men ever to have
lived, who demands that we become like him. For Paul,
to be a man is to be Christ-like and to be Christ-like is to
be a man of faith, hope and love. This must show itself in
all areas of a man's life, not least his relationships with
women.

Scholars have argued over the translation of verse 4.
The Revised Standard Version reads: 'that each of you
know how to take a *wife* for himself in holiness and
honour', but the Jerusalem Bible has 'and each one of
you know how to use the *body* that belongs to him'. Both
words, 'wife' and 'body' are suggested translations of the
Greek word *skeuos* meaning literally 'vessel'. The question is whether Paul is thinking here of 'vessel' as his wife
or his body. Against 'body' as a translation can be put the
fact that the word *ktasthai* is sometimes used of taking a
wife, and there are texts in which wives are referred to as
'vessels', eg 1 Pet 3:7. On the other hand, Paul describes
the body as a 'vessel' in 2 Cor 4:7. Either translation will
in fact serve. If we take *skeuos* as meaning a wife (RSV)
then Paul is clearly saying that wives must be loved and
honoured as persons and not exploited. On the other
hand, if it means 'body' then he is saying that the body
must be an instrument of love and honour not a means
of exploiting others—'wronging his brother in these
matters' as Paul puts it. All must behave worthily of the
Spirit who has been given to men.

Paul's advice to the Thessalonians might seem to have
an anti-missionary spirit (4:11) in recommending them to
live quietly. Should they not be actively trying to preach
christianity to their fellow-citizens and fighting against
social injustice? It has been suggested that what Paul was
warning them against was the excitement of adventism

and the view that because the end was near, all ordinary
activities could go to the winds, including Christ's precepts. But perhaps Paul is also sensitive to the charge
made against him at Thessalonica that he turned everything upside down (Ac 17:6) and feels that a repetition
of this charge would only jeopardise his work.

1. *What sort of principles should govern sexual relationships between people? Should christians take a stand
on pornography?*

2. *How far is it a christian's duty to 'turn the world
upside down'? In what circumstances is Paul's advice the
right one?*

# 5
# The coming of the Lord
# 1 Thes 4:13–5:28

**1 Thes 4:13–5:11. Death and judgement**

Although at the beginning of chapter 4 Paul suggests what is the right attitude and behaviour of a community looking forward to the *parousia*, it is at 4:13 that his real teaching on eschatology begins. The last times are vividly portrayed, but Paul's primary intention is to give a theological interpretation of this event rather than go in for literary histrionics. Verses 13–18 seem to be dealing with a problem that had grown acute in the community since his departure from Thessalonica and the writing of this letter. Perhaps some chance remark of his had contributed to it since there was an assumption that all who had received the gospel would be present at the second coming of Christ. Nothing apparently had been said about those who would die before this took place. The delay of the *parousia* and perhaps the sudden death of someone in the community may have led to doubts in the minds of some of the truth of what Paul had said. Paul has to evolve a theology of death (cf Rom 1:13 and 11:25) which is apparently new teaching to the Thessalonians. Their worry would appear to be that those who actually lived to see the *parousia* would precede those already dead in being with God in heaven (4:15).

Paul attacks, by implication, the hopelessness of the

general pagan view of death. Although many pagans did believe in some kind of an after-life, compared to Christ's promises it was a shadowy kind of existence, the end rather than the beginning. Paul wants to fill his audience with hope because the death and resurrection of Christ means that at the second coming we will begin a new and glorious existence. In his later epistles Paul emphasises that in baptism we have already begun this new existence, but this thought is not so present here. So death is seen not as an end but a transformation of life pledged to us by Christ's death and resurrection, an idea developed greatly in the story of Nicodemus in Jn 3. The event of the death and resurrection was the destruction of death and the birth of new life for the world (Gal 2:19–20 and Rom 6:3) but here the thought is rather more of this event opening the way to the new life given fully when Christ comes again. Paul is clearly trying to comfort people who are concerned about what has happened to friends and relatives who have died. They will not be forgotten at the resurrection of the dead. To us, it seems an odd problem to be worrying about, but it was real enough to the Thessalonians.

How far Paul accepted the vivid picture he paints here of the last times as literally accurate is a matter for conjecture and in the end not very important. What is important is how it is to be interpreted theologically. There seem to be two stages: first Christ descends from heaven and the dead rise from their graves. Then we, the living, are joined with them, forming a vast assembly in the heavens. Perhaps we have the beginnings here of Paul's later theology, in which he sees Christ bringing all things back to his Father, reconciling the universe to himself (Col 1:15–20). The last times (whatever they may be) will see the final triumph of good and the defeat of evil even

if, at any given moment of history, evil may appear to be
in control of man's destiny. The faith of the christian
makes him see this and hope for the future, intensifying
his love for the world.

The second half of this section is concerned with the
problem which also worried the Thessalonians; when
would this event take place? The feeling of imminence of
the *parousia* experienced by the Thessalonians was obviously unnerving. Was it akin to the edginess many
people felt at the confrontation of the United States and
Soviet Russia at the Cuba missile crisis—the feeling of
being on the brink when everything one knew might
suddenly disappear? We do not know. But Paul reminds
them that christians who live as they should need have no
fear. Even if they do not know when Christ will come
again, his coming will find them prepared because the
christian life is preparation enough. To live in faith, hope
and love is to prepare for the day of the Lord.

In using this term 'day of the Lord' Paul has taken over
something very much part of the teaching he had received
as a Jew at the feet of Gamaliel. It is a traditional term for
the day of intervention when God will defeat Israel's
enemies and set up his kingdom. It occurs first in the
prophet Amos, who proclaims that this day will also be a
day of judgment for the unredeemed world: those who
have refused to follow God's ways. Paul seems to identify
the day of the Lord (or day of Yahweh) with the second
coming of Christ (cf 1 Cor 5:5). This event will be totally
unexpected to the sinful (cf Lk 12:39 and Rev 3:3) and
as cataclysmic as any flood (Lk 17:22 and Ac 2:20). Paul
seems to suggest that the mark of the believer is that he is
a creature of the day and therefore unsurprised by the
coming of the end of things. But the sons of darkness will
be caught totally unprepared. Paul denies that salvation

is given unconditionally to the sons of light (5:6) for it is given only in so far as they have lived as followers of Christ united to his saving death. The christian is contrasted with the pagan: he is awake whereas the unbeliever is asleep. But being awake (having faith) means being prepared to discern the signs of the times, looking for the will of Christ in the world and its events, alive to the purpose of God that is to be realised in history. Such faith is to be built up in the community (cf Eph 2:22), the fellowship of believers. Perhaps we might sum up what Paul is saying by suggesting that faith demands a trans-historical view, interpreting the significance of all events in the light of the death and resurrection of Christ in the past and the fulfilment of God's creative purpose in the future, realising that whatever its shape this denouement will be of God's making.

   *1. How far is it true that there is a fear of death in our society? Is Paul's attitude to death of any help?*

   *2. How ought we to think about the* parousia? *Is it still a meaningful expression?*


## 1 Thes 5:12–28. Leadership in the community

The last part of the letter returns to the subject of the conduct of a christian community touched upon in 4:1–12. Paul begins by referring to 'those who labour among you and are over you in the Lord and admonish you'. While it would be a mistake to assume that here we have a reference to a clearly defined ministry (for example in Palestine christians may well have been still frequenting the temple and the synagogues as well as having their own forms of worship), nevertheless there is a clear reference to leaders, presumably appointed by Paul. It is interesting that the task of admonishing the idle and encouraging the weak is considered the work of the whole community, not just of its leaders (cf Mt 18), a point worth considering when thinking about the future of the parish system in this country: the leaders have the task of giving example but there is no exclusiveness in the function of encouragement and criticism. The community as a whole must not quench the Spirit nor despise prophesy. It must test everything, holding fast to what is good, because this is the task of the christian whether he be priest or layman. The decree *De Ecclesia* of the Vatican council has perhaps caught something of the flavour:

It is not only through the sacraments and Church ministries that the same Holy Spirit sanctifies and leads the People of God and enriches it with virtues. Allotting his gifts 'to everyone according as he will' (1 Cor 12:11), he distributes special graces among the faithful of every rank. By these gifts he makes them fit and ready to undertake the various tasks or offices advantageous to the renewal and upbuilding of the Church, according to the words of the Apostle: 'The manifestation of the Spirit is given to everyone for profit' (1 Cor 12:7). These charismatic gifts, whether they be the most outstanding or the more simple and widely diffused, are to be received with thanksgiving and consolation for they are exceedingly suitable and useful for the needs of the Church.

(*Documents of Vatican II*, ed Abbot, Chapman, p 30.)

*1. In what ways does the church tend to 'quench the Spirit' rather than encourage prophecy?*
*2. What should be the relationship of bishops and priests to the congregations they serve?*

# 6

## The judgement of God
## 2 Thes 1:1–42

While most scholars have accepted the authenticity of the first letter without demur, a number have doubted the Pauline authorship of the second (for details see Neil: *Thessalonians*, pp xxiff). The main problem is why Paul, if it was he, felt the need to write a second letter so soon after the first. Had some new situation arisen which had been communicated to him after the first letter had been sent? If so, it must clearly have been something to do with his teaching on eschatology, since the major portion of this letter is devoted to that subject. What is slightly odd is that again in the first four verses he thanks God for the faith and love of the Thessalonians, which seem to be growing considerably despite the afflictions and persecutions they are undergoing. That Paul accepts this as the lot of the christian is clear from this and the first letter. Suffering is an inevitable part of the christian's life as it was part of Christ's. In fact Paul goes on to suggest that the fact that they are suffering is itself evidence of the righteous judgement of God, so that by it they may become worthy of the kingdom. Faith is strengthened by adversity and suffering is the fire to temper their commitment to God. The world is ruled by the forces of darkness and so it is only to be expected that those who are faithful to the light will undergo attack (cf Mk 8:34; 13:9–13).

He who has suffered much and has given up everything for Christ's sake will receive not only the kingdom but everything back and much more (Mk 8:35; 10:23–31). But it is only when the day of the Lord comes that the righteous will receive their reward, and on that day those who have rejected Christ will be separated from him for ever.

Once again (cf 1 Thes 4:13ff) Paul depicts the day of judgement in terms very reminiscent of old testament apocalyptic. The significance of some of the details should not be missed. For example, Christ is represented as appearing from heaven with a host of angels 'in flaming fire'. Fire was a very ancient symbol of the presence of God which was constantly used in the old testament. It occurs in Gen 15:17 when God makes a covenant with Abraham. God appears to Moses under the symbol of the burning bush (Ex 3) and reveals himself at Sinai to give the covenant to the chosen people in smoke and fire (Ex 19:18; Deut 32:2). Christ also will come to his people at the end of time with these signs of his divinity and lordship over the world. But above all this event will be a revelation, in which darkness is dispelled and all things are made clear. Like Moses, men will then see God face to face, a sight which only the just will be able to bear. Those who have rejected God will suffer his vengeance and be excluded from his presence for ever (1:9) an allusion, perhaps, to Is 2:10.

How far did Paul intend all this to be taken symbolically? Despite its fearsomeness, his account is remarkably restrained by normal standards of apocalyptic writing. There are no lurid accounts of the judgement, more an emphasis on the glory of the event which is to come. Nothing more is said about the damned than that they are excluded from God's presence. Paul seems to be dividing mankind into those who are faithful to God and those who disobey or reject the gospel of the Lord Jesus. It is not ignorance of which Paul speaks when he refers to those who are to be excluded, but the desire to live in darkness, refusing the light that has been offered. The fourth gospel makes this point clear when it speaks of those men 'who loved darkness rather than light because their deeds were evil' (Jn 3:19). He seems to suggest that sin is much more the choice itself than the actual deeds we perform: what we do is consequent upon the kind of options we have made, basically whether we have accepted Christ or culpably rejected him. But how is this compatible with a God who loves all men and desires that they should be saved?

This is not an easy problem and in fact was one which occupied the minds of both old and new testament writers. The point is that we cannot choose God unless we can also reject him. We cannot love unless it is also possible for us to hate. What is slightly disturbing here is that damnation is not only pictured as a possibility but even as a likelihood for many; indeed Jesus is reported to have predicted that many would be called but few chosen. How far is this a partial understanding of the truth? The important thing here is that God is not going to force a fellowship upon men, because such a relationship would be no fellowship at all. On the other hand, is God going to allow any of his sheep to go astray?

The last two verses raise something very important in christian theology: the question of grace. Paul is very emphatic in all his writings that we cannot save ourselves; it is only Christ who can save us. The mere fact of a man becoming a christian, of answering God's call, is itself made possible by the power of God, rooted in the death and resurrection of Christ. How this is to be interpreted has been a matter of speculation by the church for centuries and many different views have been put forward. Yet all are agreed that in and through Christ something was done for man that man could not do for himself and that we now have an ability which we had not before.

*1. Can God be said to use evil and suffering to purify men?*

*2. What are we to make of the ideas of damnation and mortal sin today?*

*3. How should we understand the idea of the power of God working in men so as to avoid any sense of the magical? What is it that Christ has done for us?*

# 7

# The coming of lawlessness and the judgement of God
# 2 Thes 2:1–12

It is in this passage that Paul comes to the main point of his letter: false teaching about the second coming of Christ. It is a passage that has been much discussed by commentators and which has also provided readily accessible material for fundamentalists. Writing like this has tended to encourage prophecies of the end of the world by men living at every age since the foundation of christianity itself. Anti-Christ has been identified not only with men who persecute christians but with representatives of sects and denominations disliked by others. Nero, Henry VIII, Calvin, Stalin and the popes have all been put forward as likely candidates for the honour. The problem with this kind of writing is that it lends itself too easily to scaremongering and religious rivalry. The worst consequence of this is that there is a refusal to penetrate the biblical imagery, with the consequent obliteration of the gospel message. We have to find out just what it was that Paul was trying to say and how much was conditioned by the circumstances of the time. But having said this, it must be admitted that the passage *is* obscure because a lot is assumed by Paul in the letter which we have no means of finding out. We do not know, for example, if there had been a letter, allegedly sent by Paul, which had put a controversial and alarming view about the *parousia* (2:2). This is as likely a view as any, but we cannot be certain. It does seem safe to say, however, that considerable unrest had grown up in the Thessalonian church since his last letter and that this had centred round his teaching on the second coming. Paul had said in his first letter that some would be alive when this happened. Was this a rash remark which gave rise to further speculation causing anxiety and controversy in the community? Did they think that the *parousia* was actually at hand?

In the first part of the chapter, Paul is evidently trying to induce some sort of calm by denying that the present situation fulfils the conditions which must precede the second coming and gives them a warning very like that found in Mt 24:4. The rebellion must come first. We can probably dismiss the idea that Paul meant a political rebellion here, but like similar references in the old testament and the apocrypha it would seem to refer to a rebellion against God (Jos 22:22; 1 Mac 2:15; 2 Esdras 5:1) in which his authority is denied and flaunted to a very high degree. It does not seem to refer to the apostasy and faithlessness of individuals no matter how high their office, but to the last onslaught of evil before it is finally crushed (cf Rev 20:7–10). It will look as if evil is about to triumph.

At some stage during this rebellion the 'man of lawlessness' is revealed. The word 'man' here might be interpreted either as an individual or collectively (cf 'Adam'); it does not greatly matter which. He is a kind of Anti-Christ, although Paul does not actually use the term (cf 1 Jn 2:18 and 4:3), whose father is evil and who will attempt to usurp the rights of God even to the extent of enthroning himself in the temple. There are probably a number of old testament images and ideas contained here. One may well be the Jewish apocalyptic figure of Beliar who is progressively identified as a Satanic spirit, working many signs amongst men so as to deceive them before he is finally destroyed. The man of lawlessness enthroning himself in the temple is probably based on Dan 7:25; 8:25 and 9:36, where a wicked king is described who would put himself above every God and profane the sanctuary. He will be destroyed and God's people delivered. It is thought that what occasioned this was the action of Antiochus Epiphanes who set up an altar of Zeus in the temple at Jerusalem and which directly contributed to the Maccabean revolt of 167 BC.

Such events as this must have seemed to the Jews a sign of the nadir of their fortunes. Translated into christian terms, what Paul is suggesting is that evil must gain such a hold on men that all seems to be lost before Christ comes again to claim back what is his own. It is interesting that if the date of around 50 AD is accepted for the writing of these epistles, just ten years previously the Emperor Caligula provoked riots in Jerusalem by attempting to set up his statue in the temple. Was Paul using this as a kind of parallel or symbol of what was to happen in the future? In which case, what does he mean by 'the temple of God' (2:4)? Could this refer to the church? As the term is used in 1 Cor 3:16–17, it seems to be used in that sense. Perhaps it has cosmic significance also.

The passage seems to become even more obscure at verse 6. Who is being referred to as restraining? The word is used twice: 'restraining him now so that he may be revealed in his time' (2:6) and 'he who now restrains it will do so until he is out of the way' (2:7).

Several suggestions have been offered; the restrainer is:

(*a*) God
(*b*) Satan
(*c*) The Roman emperor Claudius, who was determined to maintain law and order.
(*d*) An angel, on analogy with Rev 20, where Satan is bound by an angel before being allowed to wreak havoc in preparation for the final defeat of evil.

Whatever suggestion is adopted, 2:9 makes it clear that the lawless one is not Satan himself but one who comes with Satan's power and with 'pretended signs and wonders'. He is the great deceiver whom only the man of faith will be able to perceive as different from Christ himself, for those who listen to him are doomed men (2:10).

At this point God is introduced as the ultimate being responsible for the whole process, since even though the man of lawlessness has been allowed full rein both he and Satan are under God's power. The man of lawlessness will be slain by the mere appearance of Christ in glory. There is a purpose behind it all; evil shall be finally routed at the moment when those who are behind it consider they are nearest to victory. Evil cannot triumph. As a punishment for faithlessness, God sends upon those who have refused to love the truth a 'strong delusion' which in effect makes them incapable of distinguishing the true from the false. They believe now what is false.

There is no doubt that this is a strange passage which raises many theological issues. But what is at least clear is that Paul does not underestimate the power of evil, which is insidious and deathly. Not only is evil, for him, a description of what men do to each other, but it is a force in the world, in man himself, which unless resisted by the man of faith brings him rapidly under its control. Evil saps at the moral fibre of a man, making him less of a man and less capable of moral decision. He is also saying that the 'man of lawlessness' situation is one in which it is very difficult to do what is right, in which the whole atmosphere and cultural ethos is working against what is good. Only a really lively faith in Christ can see a man through such a time.

*1. Is it worth trying to make anything of this sort of passage?*

*2. Does the presence of evil in the world necessarily lead to a confrontation with good?*

*3. How valid a description of evil is this?*

# 8

## God has chosen you
## 2 Thes 2:13–3:5

Abruptly at 2:13 Paul changes his tone to one of joyfulness, thanking God who has chosen the community at Thessalonica. Although this section is not meant to be a theological treatise like Galatians or Romans, much of Paul's theology is in fact implied here. What he is saying here and has already said in other parts of the two letters is that the Thessalonian christians are remarkable for their faith and so stand in marked contrast to those who refuse 'to love the truth'. Paul has something important to say here about faith: in the first instance God had chosen them before they chose him (2:13). Some versions suggest that Paul means that the Thessalonians were the first to have been chosen as christians, that they were the first christian converts: they add the words 'as the first converts' to the phrase 'God chose you from the beginning'. This however seems unlikely when we consider other passages by Paul:

> We know that in everything God works for good with those who love him, who are called according to his purpose. For those whom he foreknew, he also predestined to be conformed to the image of his Son, in order that he might be the first born among many brethren. (Rom 8:28–9.)

As he chose us in him before the foundation of the world. (Eph 1:4.)

He seems to be suggesting that faith was offered by God to those who later received it, before the foundation of the world and in the act of creation itself. Paul is propounding here in miniature some of the great doctrines he was to develop more elsewhere. This choosing of men to be saved (2:13) is a doctrine which later became known as the doctrine of predestination and election. It should be noted that this can be taken in two ways, either universally or particularly. It can mean either that God has chosen all men to be followers of him or only some and not others. By and large, the christian church has taught that God intended all men for salvation and that in Christ he has offered his grace to the world, but there are passages in Calvin, as in Islamic theology, which suggest that God has only chosen some men and rejected others. The allure of this latter view is the overtones of exclusiveness that it contains. Just as God chose the Jews and not the gentiles so he has chosen those who follow Christ but not those who reject him (or those whose views of what following Christ means differ from one's own). What this narrower view fails to see (as indeed did the Jews of Christ's time) is that God chose a people to be a means of redeeming mankind, just as he has chosen all men to be the means of reconciling each other in Christ. The church is, or should be, the sign to all men of their universal calling. What Christ did, and what the church now does, is to call all men to the realisation of their true humanity. Paul suggests that this is done in two ways: by the work of the Spirit (cf 1 Pet 1:2) and by belief in the truth, for to accept the truth of Christ is to be transformed in the Spirit. The two things which characterise a christian in

Paul's view is his commitment to Christ and God's presence in him by the Spirit, an idea which appealed greatly to Newman (cf *Parochial and Plain Sermons* ii, 19), but in a sense all this was given before creation itself. Salvation, a re-creation, was given from the beginning, but of course it only becomes actual for a particular person when that person accepts it by being united in baptism to Christ's death and resurrection (Rom 6:5). This in turn is completed when Christ comes again. In view of this, Paul exhorts them to 'stand firm and hold to the traditions which you were taught by us'. This would seem to refer to the *kerygma* and *didache*, or preaching and teaching, of the early church. What Paul means here is that they should adhere strongly to the message of Christ and the ethical teaching based upon it which he had brought to them and which was common to all the apostles and their companions. Because they had received this message from Christ, they should hold fast to it, knowing they are in the hands of God.

*1. In what sense has the church been chosen by Christ? What has it been chosen for?*

*2. How would you summarise the christian message for today? Does it share any insights with other religions or systems of thought? eg eastern religions, marxism, etc.*

# 9

# Community behaviour
# 2 Thes 3:6–17

The second major theme of this letter is the idleness of some members of the Thessalonian church. Paul's remarks on this matter may well have been meant to back up those he made in the first letter (1 Thes 4:11–12) on much the same topic. It is probable that this matter of idleness and the *parousia* were connected, in that the controversy about the day of the Lord had so unsettled some members of the community that they were not behaving responsibly but living on the charity of others without cause. Paul declares that to do this was not to live according to the tradition (preaching and teaching) that he had given them and therefore they were not living according to the gospel. Such idlers were to be ostracised.

Paul suggests that they should imitate him as an example of someone who lives according to the tradition and pay for their bread and keep. It seems to have been Paul's practice to do this, supporting himself by following his own trade, so that he could never be accused of bad motives for what he did. No one could accuse him justly of preaching for financial gain. He chose to give rather than receive. In Ac 4:32–36 we read that the Jerusalem community held all things in common, the well-off pooling their resources with the poor so that 'there was not a needy person among them'. Paul is correcting an abuse in which those who were not needy behaved as if they were. Paul seems concerned to give them an example here because he says that he is really doing without what is his due (3:9; cf Mk 10:9f) since he did accept assistance from the Philippians (Phil 4:16). He really suggests to them that what the christian does is give in love rather than receive things for himself. To do otherwise, unless there is genuine need, is to exploit others, and Paul is at pains to point out that he is against this kind of conduct in any man.

In this passage and in much of these two letters, Paul has been trying to say something about discipleship. To believe in Christ is to accept him in faith as revealed in and through the christian community. It means accepting the role of being an instrument of God's purpose in the world, of being a bringer of peace, love and justice to your fellow-men. This work does not stop even if Christ should come tomorrow because to commit oneself to Christ is to make a choice totally incompatible with selfishness or any desire to use others for your own gain. The christian must be implacably opposed to evil both within and outside the church. Paul is concerned that his community at Thessalonica should not become a scandal to the pagan citizens there but rather a way in which the message of Christ should confront the society in which they live, demanding that it should choose Christ or the man of lawlessness.

*1. What criticisms could we make of the church today in the light of this passage?*

*2. What kinds of exploitation do we find, both in the church and in society, which christians ought to oppose?*

# Galatians

*Lionel Swain*

# Introduction

Saint Paul made three major missionary journeys throughout Asia Minor and Greece, evangelising the populace and founding communities—'churches'—in many of the principal cities. During the last of these journeys, undertaken between the spring of 53 and the spring of 58, he spent some considerable time at Ephesus, from the autumn of 54 until the spring of 57. In all probability it is from here that he sent his letter to the churches of Galatia, although the precise date is the subject of much conjecture.

Galatia, properly so called, was a territory situated in the centre of Asia Minor. According to Acts, Paul passed through this region on two occasions, the first during his second missionary journey (Ac 16:6), the second during his third (Ac 18:23) although there is little suggestion in these cryptic references of the thriving communities supposed by Paul's letter. This fact, along with other considerations, has induced some scholars to include within the term 'Galatia' a much wider area of Asia Minor, evangelised by Paul during his first missionary journey, in which case the letter could have been written well before his stay in Ephesus, and could thus possibly be the earliest of his writings. This geographico-chronological discussion, however, though interesting in itself, does not affect the essential message and meaning of the work as a whole.

73

Paul's letter to the churches of Galatia was, like all his other letters, to a greater or lesser extent, of an essentially occasional character. He was no armchair theologian, but an apostle, a preacher, a shepherd of the numerous churches which he had founded, and the most profound expressions of the christian mystery which abound in his writings are less the fruit of detached reflection on the meaning of Christ than the vital response to the many and varied concrete problems occasioned by the impact of christianity upon the social, cultural, and religious structures of his day. The background against which he saw these problems was the mystery of Christ's death and resurrection and the christian's participation in it by faith and the sacraments, particularly baptism and the eucharist. It was this unique, unprecedented, unimagined, and unhoped-for fact that was the main-spring, the keystone of his thought, and all its other components, for instance the influence of contemporary cultures or his exploitation of Jewish exegetical method, have to be seen in relation to it. From this point of view alone, Galatians is an excellent example of Paul's thought and procedure.

The precise problem with which Paul was concerned in Galatians was very basic. It touched upon the essence of his teaching, his 'gospel', and his right to proclaim it, his 'apostolate'. There is a distinct polemical air about this letter. Reading between its lines, one can easily see that here, as in 1 and 2 Corinthians, written about the same time, Paul is taking to task not only the Galatians themselves but also certain persons who seem to be the real villains of the drama. These are the so-called 'judaisers', christian preachers of Jewish stock, who maintained that in order to be a christian, or at least a first-class christian, it was necessary to be, or to become, subject to all the ramifications of judaism, and to assume all the obligations of the law, at very least to undergo the rite of circumcision. It appears that they followed in Paul's wake, thus polluting his 'gospel' and, in order to render their preaching more acceptable, undermining his authority as an apostle. Their argumentation would have revolved around two main points: firstly, Paul did not derive his teaching from the divinely appointed apostolic college of Jerusalem, nor did he hold any commission from them— two claims which the 'judaisers' doubtless made for themselves; and, therefore, his message was 'from men' and not 'from God'. Secondly, his 'gospel' was manifestly invalid since it contradicted the plain teaching of the scriptures, in which the 'judaisers' considered themselves well versed.

Paul's reaction to this crisis corresponds exactly to the data of the problem. His main interest is to confirm the Galatians in the faith which they have received from him. But he knows that the argument from mere authority is not sufficient in the present circumstances, since it is precisely this authority that is being called in question. To succeed he must silence his enemies. He must tackle their objections, preferably on their own logical ground. This he does admirably, firstly by vindicating his apostolic vocation with recourse to easily verifiable incidents, and, secondly, by showing that his 'gospel', far from being contrary to the scriptures, is actually promised by them. The result is that in Galatians we have the clearest and most unforgettable affirmation both of the supreme gratuitousness of the apostolic vocation and of the christian's profound freedom in Christ.

Of all Paul's writings Galatians is probably the one which corresponds most to what is generally called a 'letter'. Here, more than elsewhere, we perceive Paul's extreme sensitivity, tenderness, spontaneity, directness and, above all perhaps, his firm conviction of the absolute character of his vocation and the grandeur of his 'gospel'. Nevertheless it would be wrong to consider Galatians as having been written 'off the cuff', or on the spur of the moment, let alone in some frenzied state of holy anger. A close attention to the literary structure of Galatians reveals that it is one of the most carefully and finely structured writings of the new testament. The modern writer conveys his thought principally by words, sentences and symbolism. The ancient writers frequently exploited a fourth means, that of the structure of the whole work, built up according to a number of well-known and easily recognisable techniques: for example, the concatenation of key words linking up the different parts of the work, the symmetrical distribution of the various propositions, the resumption at the end of a development of a word or idea given at the beginning, a process known as 'inclusion'. These are all found in Galatians in abundance. As a glance at the plan of the letter will show, apart from its introduction, 1:1–5, and the résumé and conclusion, 6:11–18, it comprises two main parts which, though ostensibly dealing with different matters, are very skilfully joined together and interrelated. Also it will be noticed that the first part consists of the alternation: rebuke–gospel–rebuke–gospel . . . , and the second of the alternation: service–Spirit–service–Spirit . . . This structure can hardly be either fortuitous or artificially superimposed by the reader, especially since it can be shown to correspond to what is evidently Paul's main aim in writing his letter. Whether it is deliberate, being the fruit of conscious literary elaboration, or undeliberate, springing from the inner structure of Paul's thought, or even the work of his secretary, after he had dictated his mind on the subject and before he put his signature to the document (6:11), is a moot point. What is certain is that this

structure is itself expressive of Paul's thought and, therefore, must be taken into consideration in any satisfactory
commentary of the letter.

*To what extent and in what ways does a consideration of
the historical setting and the method of composition used
in Galatians help us to appreciate its real meaning?*

## Plan of the epistle

1. 1:1–5: address and greeting
2. 1:6–5:12: the gospel and the law:
   (*a*) 1:6–9: rebuke
   (*b*) 1:10–2:21: defence of apostolate and gospel
   (*c*) 3:1–5: rebuke
   (*d*) 3:6–4:7: proof for the gospel
   (*e*) 4:8–11: rebuke
   (*f*) 4:12: exhortation to imitate Paul
   (*g*) 4:13–20: rebuke
   (*h*) 4:21–5:6: proof for the gospel
   (*i*) 5:7–12: rebuke
3. 5:13–6:10: from slavery to service:
   (*a*) 5:13–15: exhortation to mutual service
   (*b*) 5:16–25: exhortation to walk in the Spirit
   (*c*) 5:26–6:6: exhortation to both mutual service
   and attention to self
   (*d*) 6:7–8: exhortation to sow in the Spirit
   (*e*) 6:9–10: exhortation to universal service
4. 6:11–18: résumé and conclusion:
   (*a*) 6:11: Paul's signature
   (*b*) 6:12–17: contrast between Paul and the
   judaisers
   (*c*) 6:18: final greeting

**Book list**

1. L. Cerfaux, *The Church in the theology of St Paul.*
2. L. Cerfaux, *Christ in the theology of St Paul.*
3. L. Cerfaux, *The Christian in the theology of St Paul.*
4. C. Augrain, *Paul, Master of the Spiritual Life,* 1.
5. Jerusalem Bible.

# 1

## Address and greeting
## Gal 1:1–5

According to the current custom of his time, Paul usually begins his letters with an explicit mention of the addressees and a greeting. In Paul's case, however, this literary convention is put to the service of the christian message, the stereotyped formulae being charged with new meaning as they are developed in the light of the fundamental kerygma. In the present instance it also serves to introduce, and to sum up, the central theme of the letter. Paul attributes to himself the title of 'apostle', a term used in the new testament to designate specifically the 'twelve' (Lk 6:12). He is justifiably proud of this title and uses it frequently of himself throughout his letters, but in the context of the Galatian crisis it is invested with a certain apologetic slant: Paul is just as much an 'apostle' as the other apostles in Jerusalem (1:17). Moreover, this apostolate is neither of human origin, nor mediated through men, but comes directly from Jesus Christ and the Father. Paul is obviously here implicitly evoking the charges of his adversaries, but, as the development of the letter will show, he includes within the phrase 'not from men, nor through man' the Jerusalem apostles themselves (1:16–17). The judaisers had argued from his notoriously slight contact with the mother church to the purely human character of his mandate. Paul uses the same argument to

79

prove its divine character. After all, had he been commissioned merely by the Jerusalem community he would
not be an apostle of Christ, in the fullest sense of that
term. To substantiate the claim to be on the same pedestal
as the 'twelve' it was necessary to show that he too had experienced direct contact with the risen Christ, the first
requisite for being an apostle (1:15–16; 1 Cor 15:8–9).
Paul's claim was far more daring than even the judaisers
had suspected, and their very accusations served only to
deepen his awareness of it and to provoke him to express
it in such poignant terms.

Similarly, the twofold mention of Christ's death (1:1
and 4) is not without polemical overtones. Both Paul's
apostolate and the 'grace' and 'peace' which he wishes for
his readers (1:3) have their origin in the sacrificial death
(1:4) and the resurrection (1:1) of the Father's Son. This
saving death and resurrection of Christ into which the
christian is introduced by faith and baptism is repeatedly
contrasted throughout the rest of the letter with the radical ineffectiveness of the Jewish law to save or 'justify'
man (2:16–20; 3:1–3, 12–13; 5:11; 6:12–16). Moreover,
the salvation offered by Christ is different not only in
degree but also in kind from that attributed to the Jewish
law. It is a redemption from the 'present evil age', which
includes this law as one of its structures (1:1; 4:3, 9–10).
It involves, therefore, a passage from the old world to the
new creation (6:15). Thus from the very outset Paul in a
sure, albeit implicit, allusive, and evocative way spikes his
adversaries' guns by reminding his readers of the essence
of the apostolate and the kernel of the gospel message.
The rest of the letter might very well be considered as a
persistent drawing out of the implications contained in
the first five verses or, to continue the martial image, an
all-out attack on the enemy.

*1. Show how this section resumes the contents of the whole epistle.*

*2. Does Paul's idea of the 'apostolate' have any bearing on contemporary discussions around this subject?*

# 2

# The gospel and the law
# Gal 1:6–5:12

### (a) Gal 1:6–9. Rebuke

Paul usually begins his letters with profuse praise for his readers' faith or a prayer for their continuance therein. Both of these are remarkably absent from Galatians, since the news which Paul has received concerning the recently founded communities provides little motive for them in his eyes. Instead he frankly rebukes these communities for their desertion of the Father (1:6). It is interesting to notice, in this connection, the role which Paul ascribes to each of the persons of the Trinity in this letter, which is markedly 'trinitarian' in structure. The Father is both the ultimate source of salvation (1:1, 4, 6, 16; 3:8, 18; 4:4, 9) and its final end (1:5, 13, 24; 2:19; 3:11; 4:6; 5:21; 6:7, 16). He is designated mostly by the term 'God', but 'the Father' is used in 1:1, 3, 4, probably not without polemical intent, since the whole movement of the letter receives its climax in 4:6 where Paul shows that the real dignity of the christian is to be, not a carnal descendant of Abraham, as absolute adherence to the Jewish law would seem to imply, but rather a spiritual child, which means ultimately being a son, not of Abraham, but of God. Salvation is therefore a matter of divine adoption (4:5). This God the Father effects in and through his Son, Christ, who is thus the mediator of salvation (1:1, 4, 6, 12, 16;

2:4, 16–20; 3:14, 22, 26, 28; 5:6; 6:14). Finally it is the Spirit who, through faith, transforms the christian into the image of the Son (3:2, 5, 14; 4:6, 19, 29; 5:5) and enables him to live the life of the Son (5:16–25; 6:8). This 'trinitarian' perspective: from the Father, through the Son, in the Spirit—in the Spirit, through the Son, to the Father, is the most universalistic conceivable and contrasts strikingly with the particularist view of the judaisers who insisted on mediation through the Jewish law.

The whole of Christ's saving work, accomplished at a certain point of time, is 'realised', re-presented, in Paul's preaching, in his 'gospel'. This word, therefore, designates more than a book. It is the work of salvation actualised in the apostolic preaching: the gospel *of Christ*, that is, the gospel *which is* Christ (1:7). Thus Paul emphatically affirms the oneness and the immutability of the gospel, insisting on the importance of tradition. For the gospel has its origin, not in abstract speculation on the meaning of the scriptures, but in the unique Christ-event which is not subject to change, even though it is susceptible of an infinite variety of interpretations and representations. Now in its essential, stark reality it is incompatible with the judaisers' thesis—a point which Paul will elaborate throughout the letter. In a word, Paul's gospel is a gospel of 'grace' (1:6 and 7; 2:21) and not of the law (2:21).

*1. What does this section tell us about the unity of the gospel?*

*2. What are the dangers, if any, to that unity in the world today?*

*3. Discuss the trinitarian structure of this section.*

## (b) Gal 1:10–2:21. Defence of apostolate and gospel

One of the accusations of Paul's adversaries was doubtless that he had a vested interest in his gospel, that he preached in order to gain men's favour. He thus begins his apology by recalling that there was indeed a time when he did try to please men, that is, during his life as a devout Jew, but that he has abandoned this ambition in order to become a 'slave' of Christ (1:10). In the context of a letter which is centred on the antithesis slavery-freedom, this expression has particular significance. The slavery in question is that of the law (2:4; 4:1, 3, 7, 21–31; 5:1). Paul knows better than anyone the radical opposition between the Jewish law, considered as absolute, and Christ, since he was at one time so far committed to it as to persecute Christ in its name (1:13). By his conversion he had changed camps. From the persecutor he had become the persecuted. Was this to court human favour? On the contrary, to suffer persecution is a sure sign both of the disinterestedness of Paul and of the authenticity of his gospel (6:14). Paul's conversion is an eloquent testimony to the power of the gospel and its transcendence over the narrow confines of judaism. That is why he can sum up his thought on the gospel by pointing to his own example: 'Brethren, I beseech you, become as I am, for I also have become as you are' (4:12). On the other hand, with his insistence on his radical conversion and the ensuing persecution he subtly suggests that the real suitors of human favour are none other than the judaisers themselves (6:12), who are attempting to reverse the process of his conversion.

Paul now proceeds to drive his point home by underlining both the divine origin of his gospel and his radical independence vis-à-vis the members of the apostolic college in Jerusalem (1:11–24). Whereas the Galatian churches have 'received' the gospel from Paul (1:9), Paul declares that he has not 'received' it from any man, but that it came to him through a 'revelation of Jesus Christ' (1:12), that is, a revelation which had Christ as its object (1:15). He does not necessarily deny here that he had knowledge of the christian faith before his conversion or that he underwent some form of catechetical instruction after his conversion. He is merely asserting that what was specific in his preaching, that is, justification by faith in Christ, was the object not of tradition but of a direct revelation of the Father in him. Nor does this affirmation imply opposition between Paul and the Jerusalem apostles, since he will soon emphasise the fundamental agreement on this very point between himself and his confrères (2:1–10). It is worth pointing out, however, that it was this revelation and the subsequent missionary experience of Paul which contributed considerably to the recognition of the truth by the Jerusalem church (2:7–9; Ac 15:3, 12).

The judaisers were not attacking someone who was ignorant of judaism. Far from it. Paul has trodden every inch of the road along which the judaisers are inviting the Galatians to accompany them, and knows from experience that it is a dead end. There is a note of irony in these words (1:13–14) which recurs as a *leitmotiv* throughout the rest of the letter where more than once Paul shows his profound grasp both of the scriptures and of rabbinical exegetical technique. Anything the judaisers can do he can do better. Even the reminiscence of his vocation is couched in terms which evoke the great prophetical figures of the old testament, Jeremiah (Jer 1:5) and the servant of Yahweh (Is 49:1, 5). This turning point in his life occurs not as the climax of his zeal for the law, to which it is opposed, but out of the purely gratuitous decision of the Father. Nor is it a mere chance happening, but a moment for which he has been destined 'from his mother's womb'. His life in judaism was, therefore, only a phase calculated to pass away at a time willed by the Father, just as the Jewish law itself had but a temporary role to play in the whole economy of salvation (3:19–4:7). Thus Paul experienced in himself, in the drama of his own conversion, the whole history of salvation in miniature. This thought brings out the nuance of the original Greek 'in me' (1:16). Paul preached the gospel, not merely by word of mouth, but also by his very existence. He does not divide his christian life into two compartments, the one marked 'christian', the other 'apostle'. His conversion *was* his vocation and vice versa (4:12).

The mention of 'flesh and blood' (1:16) in the present context evokes Christ's words to Peter in Mt 16:17: 'Blessed are you, Simon Bar-Jona. For *flesh and blood* has not *revealed* this to you, but my *Father* who is in heaven.' In both cases it is a matter of a supernatural revelation by the Father of his Son forming the basis of the apostolate. Paul did not derive his knowledge of Christ from 'flesh and blood' any more than Peter did before him. He is an apostle in his own right and, therefore, had no need to consult those who were apostles 'before' him (1:17).

There is some discrepancy between the events succeeding Paul's conversion as they are recorded in Galatians, on the one hand, and in Acts on the other. In general, since in the Acts we are very often presented with Luke's reading and ordering of the events to suit his own purposes, it seems more reasonable to follow Paul's own account. It is only here (1:17) that there is any mention of a stay in Arabia. What did Paul do there? It is tempt-

ing to think of him as the first christian retreatant preparing for his future apostolate with a time of recollection
and prayer, as his master before him (Mt 4:1–11), but this
idea has no real basis in the text, and it is more probable
that he went to the inhabited parts of Arabia and simply
preached the gospel there.

Even when, after three years (1:18), Paul did go up to
Jerusalem to visit Peter his stay was very brief and his
contacts with the community there extremely limited, not
sufficient to form the basis of his gospel. The only knowledge which the communities of Judea had of him at that
time was by reputation (1:23–24). The journey mentioned in 1:21 is undoubtedly his first missionary journey
(spring 45–spring 49).

Having defended his independence in relation to the
Jerusalem apostles Paul goes on to stress the fundamental
agreement regarding his gospel among the apostolic college as a whole (2:1–10). The figure of fourteen years
should be taken as approximate, just as the preceding
figure of three years (1:18), and cannot be used as a reliable basis for establishing the chronology of Paul's life.
The idea that Paul wishes to convey is that his gospel was
not only revealed to him directly by God, but has also had
a considerable running-in period before ever it was communicated to the Galatian communities, and all this independently of the Jerusalem apostles. He also emphasises
that he did not go up to Jerusalem as a subordinate,
rendering an account of his commission to superiors. He
went there by 'revelation' (2:2), that is, under the initiative of the Father (1:15). Nevertheless we have here a
witness to the central position which Jerusalem held in
his thought. He always considered it to be the mother
church (4:26) and in the present context sees the necessity
of its assent to his mission. He did not see the need to ex-

plain his behaviour to the whole community, but only to those who 'were of repute' (2:2, 6), that is, his brother apostles. This must be one of the earliest texts illustrating the doctrine of episcopal collegiality. In fact the occasion in question was most probably the first council in the history of the church, the synod of Jerusalem, held in about 49 (Ac 15:1–31). At this most important meeting the main question discussed was precisely the one which occupies Paul here: the exact relationship between christianity and judaism. A decision was reached not by deduction from a set of abstract principles, but by induction from God's revealed action: God himself had shown, particularly by the startling conversion of the Roman centurion Cornelius (Ac 10:1–11:18; 15:7–11, 14) and the missionary activity of Paul (Ac 13:46–48; 14:27; 15:3, 4, 12) that all men, regardless of their race, culture or religion, are called to belong to the new religion of Jesus Christ, that the only requirement for entry into the kingdom of God is faith expressed in baptism. This principle was quite clearly enunciated in the letter recorded in Ac 15:23–29 and it is somewhat strange that Paul does not refer explicitly to this document and thus dispense himself from a great deal of subtle argumentation. Some of those who take Galatia in the wide sense use this difficulty as a proof for their thesis and hold that Galatians was written before the council of Jerusalem, the episode referred to in the letter not being the council at all. It seems more probable, however, that we are dealing with one and the same event and that the difficulty is solved either by the fact that the letter in question was sent some considerable time after the council, and later inserted by Luke in its present context, or by the fact that the letter, issued soon after 49, was not circulated in Galatia properly so-called. Fortunately for succeeding christian generations, Paul did not simply refer his correspondents to their church archives. It is also noticeable that Paul mentions only one stipulation made by the Jerusalem apostles, that of consideration for the 'poor' (2:10), which is not stated in Acts. Paul spent a great deal of his energy on the organisation of a collection for the 'saints' in Jerusalem (2 Cor 8–9; Rom 15:25–29) regarding it as an act of religious homage paid to the mother church.

With 2:3–4 we meet the first real indications concerning the precise content of Paul's gospel. As could be expected in a context in which Paul argues from concrete occurrences, the gospel itself is exemplified in a person, this time Titus, the disciple and companion of Paul. Being of gentile stock, he should have been circumcised, according to the judaisers' thesis. In fact the Jerusalem apostles had neither demanded nor advised this, a sure sign that they recognised Paul's gospel in the person of Titus. On the other hand, Paul points out that the origin of the judaising tendency is to be found among certain 'false brethren' (2:4). Moreover this movement is characterised by 'slavery' as opposed to 'freedom' (cf 4:21–31). Had Paul not fought against this tendency, and his point not been recognised by the rest of the apostolic college, the Galatians would not have had the 'truth' of the gospel preached to them in the first place (2:5).

The final result of the council of Jerusalem, as far as Paul was concerned, was that his apostolate to the gentiles was recognised to be as authentic as Peter's to the circumcised, that is, the Jews (2:6–9). The impression given by this decision, however, could be that there were two gospels, the one to the Jews, the other to the gentiles. The point of recalling the Antioch incident seems to be to prove that in fact there is only one gospel for Jew and gentile alike (2:11–21). In the previous episode it was a matter of circumcision (2:3). Here it is a matter of the Jewish alimentary laws (2:12) which still constituted a dividing line between Jew and gentile. Peter had obviously not seen the full implications of the council's decision or, at least, did not have the courage of his convictions. At any rate Paul considered his 'insincerity' (2:13) as a dangerous compromise of the gospel's truth (2:14). Peter's eating with the gentiles symbolised his communion with them. His 'separation' from them (2:12) was a sign that he considered them to be 'unclean', whereas he knew from his own experience (Ac 10:15; 15:6–11) that all men were equal in God's sight, that the barrier erected by the accumulation of Jewish laws between Jews and gentiles was artificial and accessory and destined to be demolished (Eph 2:14–15). As far as he was concerned, therefore, his behaviour at Antioch was 'hypocritical' (2:13), a failure to live up to his principles. As far as the others, that is, the rest of the Jews, especially Barnabas (2:13)—not to mention the mass of gentiles (2:12)—were concerned, it was a scandal.

It is the Antioch affair, which, although recorded only here, must have been widely publicised, that provides the occasion for the formulation not just of *Paul's* gospel but of *the* gospel (2:14–21). Paul reminds Peter that redemption in Christ means not simply non-circumcision and exemption from Jewish practices for the gentiles but even for the Jews themselves, that the Jewish religion has been superseded and transcended by the new religion of Christ, in which there are no longer the divisions and distinctions based on the natural differences of race, social status and sex which were so pronounced in the Jewish law (3:28; 6:15). Corresponding to this new religion is a new means of access to the Father: faith in Jesus Christ (2:16) sealed by baptism (3:27), opposed to the 'works of the law'

(2:16). As usual, Paul's argument is based primarily on
christian experience. It is only incidentally, and in order
to illustrate and drive home his point, that he has recourse
to other kinds of argument, that is, scriptural and legalistic. It is interesting to notice the gradation in his thought
here (2:14–21): 'you' (Peter), 2:14; 'we' (converts from
judaism), 2:15–17; 'I' (Paul), 2:18–21. In each case it is a
question of an appeal to the christian experience of
redemption in Christ, seen as being opposed to and
transcending the law, culminating in the spontaneous
testimony of Paul himself.

The words used in the present context to describe the
reality of christian redemption are the key pauline terms
of 'life—to live' (2:19, 20) and 'justice—to be justified'
(2:16, 17, 21). Both of these ideas must be seen in the light
of their original biblical setting. 'Life' for the old testament and judaism was far more than a biological pheno-
menon. It was a qualitative fulness of being, transcending
merely material existence, in fact a participation in the
very being of God who alone is 'living' in the fullest sense
of the word (Deut 5:26). Similarly, though originally a
forensic notion, 'justice' is revealed in the bible as one of
God's fundamental attributes, in fact synonymous with
his saving love (Is 1:27) and thus 'to be just' means to
share in God's justice. Moreover there is in the old testament a very close connection between 'life', 'justice', and
the law. It was by keeping the commandments that a person both lived (Deut 8:3) and was just or justified (Ps 119:
106). It would be wrong to overlook or minimise the
genuineness of the sentiments expressed in these and many
similar passages of the old testament. In a way difficult for
us to understand the devout Jew really experienced union
with God in keeping the commandments (Ps 119). It is
therefore, in a sense, true to say that the law did give

life and justice. In order to appreciate the exact tenor of Paul's argumentation it is absolutely necessary to realise that he does not set out to give a complete picture of the law-justification relationship. He adopts an essentially apologetical stance and, like all the rabbis of his time and Christ himself, chooses and exploits to the full the biblical texts which sustain his thesis, regardless, for the most part, of their original contexts and of the fact that, taken on their own, they represent only a partial view of the subject. Were Paul dealing with this question dispassionately, his treatment would be far more nuanced. With his strong command of the scriptures he could express the christian message positively in Jewish legalistic terms. Even in this letter he speaks of fulfilling the 'law' (5 : 14; 6 : 2). But here he is reacting violently against those who ascribe too absolute and permanent a character to the law. Against these he quotes Ps 143 : 2, relating it to 'the works of the law' whereas in its original context there is no mention at all of the law. Nevertheless this use of the scripture is more than a brilliant display of pedantry. It serves to emphasise the fact that even if the law did give life and justice, this was only typologically and in relation to Christ, the fulfilment of the law. Once the antitype and the reality has arrived, there is no longer room for the type and the shadow.

To look for 'life' and 'justice' in the law—or in anything else, for that matter—after Christ is implicitly to deny the definitive effectiveness of his redemptive work (2 : 21), worse, to make Christ the agent of sin from which 'justification' is necessary (2 : 17). It is in fact to destroy the whole meaning of christianity, since the christian by faith and baptism, uniting him to Christ (2 : 20), has died to the law through the law (2 : 19). Here again it is necessary to recognise the polemical character, and therefore the limited and relative scope, of Paul's arguments. He obviously has in mind the events leading up to the condemnation and death of Christ. According to the gospel tradition, here corroborated by Paul, these were due to the rejection and excommunication of Christ by official judaism, epitomised by the 'law' (Jn 19:7). Christ, therefore, died through, or according to the law. But this death, being the ultimate exclusion from judaism, meant death *to* the law, that is, being placed outside the law. Now in fact it was from this outlaw condition that Christ rose to a new life. Paul sees a causal connection between these two phases: death to the law and life to God. Christ died to the law *in order* to live to the Father. It follows from this that the religion of Christ is essentially a religion of death to the law, of radical separation from it. This death takes place for the christian at his baptism which is a conformity to Christ's death (Rom 6:3). But baptism leaves the christian very much *in* the flesh (2:20), if not *of* it. The implication here is that life according to the law was a life according to the flesh (3:3). This way of life, however, has now been put aside, 'killed' in fact, to make place for faith in Christ. Faith for Paul is more than notional assent to the truth of the incarnation. It is a complete surrender to, and reliance upon, the person of Christ. Hence he can speak of this faith as the life of Christ within him (2:20; Phil 1:21). All that pious Jews, Paul himself at one time included, experienced in the keeping of the law, he now experiences in a supreme and transcendent way in the person of Christ.

Paul began this section with the defence of his apostolate and his gospel. Towards the end he has moved imperceptibly to a consideration of the gospel in its relation to the law. The rest of the first part of the letter will consist in a development of this point from different angles.

*1. Would you analyse the conversion of Paul in psychological terms?*

*2. Is it possible to separate his conversion from his vocation, and to what extent is the intimate connection between these two realities realised in all christians?*

*3. Does Paul's insistence on the divine origin and transcendence of the gospel have any importance for twentieth-century christianity?*

## (c) Gal 3:1–5. Rebuke

Having reminded the Galatians of the meaning of the gospel, Paul now proceeds to upbraid them for their 'stupidity' in not seeing its clear incompatibility with judaism (3:1). This reproach is all the more cutting in that it is probably a sarcastic reference to the pretended 'gnosis' of the judaisers and their followers. Paul is here addressing himself not to those familiar with the Jewish tradition, but to christians of gentile origin. His appeal is therefore not to the Jewish aspirations after 'life' and 'justice' (2:16) but to the more immediately experiential reception of the Spirit and its effects (3:2–5). The communication of the Spirit was frequently accompanied by exterior manifestations in the early church (Ac 2:1–4; 8:14–19; 10:44–47; 1 Cor 12). To accept the law after this reception of the Spirit is to end up with the flesh (3:3; 2:20).

*1. What sort of manifestations of the Spirit could Paul have had in mind here?*

*2. How is the Spirit manifested in the church today?*

*3. Is Paul's apologetic argument here meaningful for us today?*

## (d) Gal 3:6–4:7. Proof for the gospel

The judaisers prided themselves on being the children,
or 'seed' of Abraham (3:7, 16, 19, 29) and doubtless
offered this privilege to their prospective converts.
Against them Paul shows that the true descendants of
Abraham are those, the gentiles included (3:8), who have
faith, Abraham's only real claim to distinction being his
faith (3:6; Gen 15:6). It was this faith that constituted
him as father of God's people, that justified him (3:6;
3:16). Like father, like son. To be a true child of
Abraham it is necessary to share his faith (3:7). Mere
carnal descent is not enough (Mt 3:9; Jn 8:33–59). There
must be a spiritual descent (3:3). The idea of carnal
descent is related immediately to birth within the Jewish
race, but also has obvious overtones of the circumcision
rite, performed in the 'flesh', by which Jewish males were
integrated into the Jewish religious community, and
which was being offered to the Galatians by the judaisers
(2:3, 7, 8, 9; 4:21–31; 5:2, 3, 11, 12; 6:12, 13, 15). It is
only to such spiritual progeny that the blessing promised
to Abraham will be communicated (3:9).

Arguing in a typically rabbinical fashion, Paul shows
that, contrary to *faith* which pronounces *blessing*, the
*works of the law* spell out a *curse* (3:10). Similarly he
points out precisely why the law cannot justify: because
justification arrives only through faith (3:11) and the law
does not rest on faith (3:12). The operative word in 3:12
is 'does' (Lev 18:5) and Paul obviously reads far more
into it than its original context suggests. As an abstract
principle 'life through the *observance* of the commandments' is all very well. But it does make that life depend
upon *action* (3:2) and experience shows that it is virtually
impossible to observe all the commandments. Life

through them is, therefore, virtually impossible. Faith, however, is less a matter of personal *action* than openness to the action of another, reliance, that is, on the person of Christ (Jn 6:28–29). It is in fact Christ who is the agent of justification.

3:13–14 express essentially the same thought as 2:19–20. There Paul had intimated that the rejection and excommunication of Christ had been the *cause* of his death. Here he shows that they are its *effect*. Even supposing that Christ had not been condemned and executed as a criminal, the mere fact of his having been 'hanged on a tree' (Deut 21:33) meant that he was to be considered 'impure', 'accursed by God', in other words, beyond and outside the law. The two facts that all who rely on the law are 'under a curse' (3:10) and that Christ by his death 'became a curse' (3:13) are interrelated by Paul in terms of the 'redemption'. In order to understand Paul's thought here it is necessary to bear in mind the cultural background against which he is writing. In particular, the word 'curse' has to be seen in its correct setting. Here it is used in its strictly Jewish legalistic and cultic sense. Paul is even careful to omit the reference to God in the original text of Deuteronomy: 'for a hanged man is accursed *by God*'. It means that Christ by the very fact of his death on the cross has been put outside the 'blessing' of the law, that he has become, as far as official judaism is concerned, something worse even than the gentile nations. This condition obviously corresponds to the value attributed to the law and official judaism. Paul is not slow to show that in fact it is a 'blessing in disguise'. For being outside the law means for Christ that he is no longer under the law, no longer under its curse. But this state has a meaning for others also (3:13). The expression 'for us' does not denote mere vicarious substitution: Christ became a curse *in our place,* dispensing us, as it were, from becoming a curse ourselves. Nor is it a matter of his having assumed this state merely 'in our favour', on our behalf. It is essentially a matter of *solidarity* with Christ. To be properly understood the phrase 'for us' must be seen in the context of the letter as a whole in which real union with Christ by faith and baptism is clearly emphasised (2:20; 3:27–28; 4:19; 5:6). If the christian is 'in Christ' and Christ in him (2:20), then it follows that if Christ is outside the law, so is he. To describe this process which takes place in Christ Paul uses the verb 'to redeem'. This word means literally 'to buy' or 'to buy back' and is a term of commerce, particularly of the pawn shop or slave market variety. Doubtless Paul uses it to express the passage from slavery to freedom which has occurred in Christ (5:1). It is the *fact* of christian freedom, or, more precisely, of the christian's having been freed, that suggests this image to Paul. Thus the notion of 'redemption' is a finishing not a starting point. Moreover it is only one notion among many others used to express the meaning of Christ's mystery. If the word 'redemption' has come to be synonymous with this mystery, it needs constantly to be recalled that the *reality* which it describes is far richer and more complex than the meaning of the actual word.

It is only because Christ is outside the law that he is able to receive the blessing promised to Abraham, that is, the blessing of all *nations,* all those who, by their condition, are *outside the law,* and in so doing he becomes the mediator of that blessing for all the nations. Thus the *'in you'* of Gen 12:3 is realised *'in Christ'* (3:14). In the following verses Paul will show how this is consonant with the scriptures.

3:15–18 provide an excellent specimen of Paul's rabbinical exegesis, in which he combines two ideas, the one

taken from legal practice, the other from the text of
Gen 12:7. In both cases there is a play on words. The
Greek term which Paul uses for a 'will'—*diathēkē*—
(3:15) is exactly the same as that used for 'covenant'
(3:17; 4:24; Heb 9:16–17) although the two notions are
obviously quite different. Although the original word in
Gen 12:7—'seed'—refers to Abraham's descendants considered as a multitude, Paul fastens on to the singular
form, applying it to Christ (3:16). Obviously he can do
this only because he knows that in fact the promises made
to Abraham were fulfilled in Christ (3:14). Paul's exegesis
was no more disinterested than that of any contemporary
rabbi. In his application of these ideas to the case in
point, Paul emphasises the primacy of the 'promise' over
the 'law' (3:17–18) and introduces the theme of 'inheritance' (3:18) which dominates the rest of this section
(3:29; 4:1, 7).

Before developing the theme of inheritance, however,
Paul must answer an obvious question: 'What, then, is
the point of the law?' (3:19). In doing this he brings out
both the negative and the positive aspect of the law. Here
(3:19, 21–22), as in 2:19 and 3:13 he argues from a fact
to a causal relationship. Although the law, considered as
God's gift, is not in itself contrary to his promises (3:21),
and could thus, *in theory*, be both life-giving and justifying, *in fact* it has been the vehicle of transgressions (3:19)
and sin (3:22). The effect of the law has been to turn sin
into the transgression of a commandment, to heighten
therefore man's consciousness of sin, to multiply its possi-
bilities, to make it easier. The law is at the service of sin
(Rom 4:15; 5:20; 7:7). But Paul sees in this fact a provi-
dential arrangement by God. Clearly if the effect of the
law were merely negative it would contravene God's
beneficence. He would be shown to be some kind of

supernatural sadist. The law, however, is only temporary and essentially related to the future. Even the consciousness of sin which it gives enables man to see his profound need of redemption, which can come only as a free gift in Christ (Rom 7:24–25). Providentially orientated towards the future (3:19, 22), the law has thus a positive value which Paul explains by comparing it with the role of the pedagogue in the society of his time (3:23–24).

Given this temporary and educative role of the law, once Christ and faith has come (3:24, 25) the law has become obsolete, since the fulness of redemption, that is, divine sonship, has been obtained through faith in Christ (3:26). The restrictive force of the law, based on the distinctions of race, social condition, and sex, has been destroyed, since 'all are one in Christ Jesus' (3:28). Faith and baptism in Christ have thus a liberating power to which there corresponds a new law and a new morality. Few texts of the new testament express as clearly as 3:27–29 the realism of the union with Christ achieved in faith and baptism, a union which forms the basis of divine sonship and inheritance (3:29; 4:7).

Even in this discussion of the purpose of the law Paul turns the knife in his adversaries' wounds by reminding his readers, in parenthesis, of the inferior character of the law in relation to the promise (3:19–20). According to rabbinical tradition the law was given to Moses by angels, whereas the promise was given to Abraham directly by God.

In 4:1–7 Paul provides a synthesis of his thought on the relation between the law and Christ in terms of a will and the inheritance which it contains (3:15–18). Already in 3:28 he has passed sentence on the purely arbitrary laws concerning the natural distinctions of race, social status, and sex. In 4:3 he reminds his readers of another form of slavery to which the Jewish law would subject them, a slavery, that is, to the Jewish alimentary laws and system of feasts, based on purely natural phenomena, described here as the 'elements of the world'. Until the advent of Christ all men, the Jews included, had been en-slaved to these elements in so far as their relationships with God had been conditioned by them almost ex-clusively. But now in Christ, the Son, a new relationship to God has been revealed, that of a child towards its father. Whereas the natural distinctions of race, social status, sex, and times and seasons (4:10) are susceptible of a great deal of complicated elaboration, superstition even, the state of childhood is the most simple and universal possible. Paul insists that this divine adoption is not a chance happening but the climax of a long preparation enveloping the whole course of history: 'when the fulness of time had come' (4:4). The trinitarian structure of 4:4–6 is very clear. The initiative in the work of redemp-tion (4:5) comes from the Father. The Son is the media-tor and the work is finally accomplished in the Spirit. It is also interesting to notice the whole movement of God's redemptive plan clearly expressed: *from* the Father, *through* the Son, *in* the Spirit—*through* the Son, *to* the Father. The end of redemption is explicit recognition by men of God as their Father. The originality of the chris-tian revelation in this regard is that the 'Father' in ques-tion is not just God considered as creator, or even the God of the old testament seen as entering into a special fatherly relationship with his people, but the Father of Jesus Christ. By faith and baptism the christian becomes the child not of the Trinity but of the first person of the Trinity. This truth is vividly expressed by the quotation of part of an early christian prayer: 'Abba, Father!' (4:6), which is found on Christ's own lips in Mk 14:36. It expresses the unique relationship between Christ and his Father in a way that no other formula of contemporary Jewish prayer could do. The significance of its being found on the lips of the baptised is that the christian is a child of God in a sense which completely transcends anything that judaism could offer. The christian is by adoption what Christ is by nature. The 'spirit' in question is obviously the Holy Spirit, the third person of the Trinity, but he is revealed here as the Spirit of the Son, the Spirit of the promise (3:14), the Spirit of freedom (4:7), that is, his role in the work of redemption is emphasised. In 2:19 and 3:13 Paul related redemption to Christ's death. Now he associates it with his birth (4:4–5). Christ was definitely 'under the law' before being outlawed. He became like us so that we may become like him, and to do that we must share in his passage from subjection to the law to freedom from the law, that is, from death to life, through death in Christ by baptism.

*1. Discuss the various images which Paul uses in this section to illustrate his point.*

*2. What are the essential differences between a Jewish and a christian understanding of the old testament?*

*3. How is the uniqueness of the gospel to be related to the call to all nations?*

## (e) Gal 4:8–11. Rebuke

Having given a positive exposition of the gospel, Paul now shows the significance of the Galatians' wish to subscribe to the tenets of judaism as well as its utter absurdity, emphasising once more the initiative of the Father in redemption (4:9).

*1. Discuss the relationship between christian freedom and liberation.*

*2. Is it possible to draw a parallel between the complexities of judaism in Paul's time and the laws of the church today?*

### (f) Gal 4:12. Exhortation to imitate Paul

Paul now tries a more personal approach to his Galatian readers, pleading with them to imitate him. In fact his conversion and subsequent life were an admirable living commentary on the gospel which he preached. His readers are for the most part of gentile origin, that is, outside the law. By his conversion Paul had placed himself outside the law, had become, therefore, as the gentiles.

*What does this passage tell us about Paul's conception of the apostolate and what message does it contain for the modern apostle?*

### (g) Gal 4:13–20. Rebuke

Continuing this personal note, Paul recalls the circumstances in which he first preached the gospel to the Galatians, rebuking them with corresponding gentleness and finesse. 4:19 is a magnificent description of the apostolic role (1 Cor 4:15) and forms the basis of his appeal to the Galatians to imitate him as a child should its father.

*Is this section any more than an effusion of oriental sentiment?*

### (h) Gal 4:21–5:6. Proof for the gospel

After this brief cease-fire Paul launches another exegetical attack, this time addressing himself directly to the juda-

isers, or at least to the more dissident members of the
Galatian communities. 4:21–31 present the finest example of allegorical exegesis in the new testament. To
understand the passage it is necessary to realise that Paul
does not intend to give an inspired, authoritative interpretation of Genesis. He uses it merely to substantiate his
thesis. Starting from the experienced fact of christian
freedom in the Spirit and the continued existence of
judaism, he sets out to explain this situation in the light
of the old testament. Since 3:6 his mind has been occupied with the idea of Abraham and the promise. In fact
the first realisation of the promise made to Abraham was
the birth of Isaac from his true wife as opposed to the
birth of Ishmael from his slave girl Hagar. This opposition: Isaac, son of *the promise*—Ishmael, son of a *slave
girl* provides the basis for Paul's allegory. Upon it Paul
superimposes the idea of the two covenants compared to
women and, more particularly, the idea of the city of
Jerusalem compared to a mother (4:26–27). He is thus
able to build up a neat parallelism between Hagar and
Mount Sinai on the one hand, and Sarah and the heavenly
Jerusalem on the other, and to apply to the contemporary
situation the injunction of Gen 21:10–12 (4:30).

Slavery and freedom are incompatible. The law represents the one, Christ the other (5:1). To subscribe to the
law after Christ is therefore to revert to a situation of
slavery. Paul goes on to show that there can be no question of compromise in this matter. To receive circumcision symbolises commitment to the observance of the
whole law. And as he has already shown (3:11–12), it is
virtually impossible to keep the whole law. Further, to
seek justification through the law is implicitly to deny the
purely gratuitous gift of justification in Christ, which has
yet to be fully achieved (5:5). For the present the essence

of the christian life is faith expressed in, and working through charity, that is, love (5:6).

*Compare Paul's allegory with the historical account of Abraham and his two wives. How far is Paul 'true' to the original meaning of the Genesis account and how far does he go beyond it?*

## (i) Gal 5:7–12. Rebuke

Paul ends the first part of his letter, as he began, with a rebuke (5:8–9), but also with a note of optimism (5:10). He reminds his readers of the radical opposition between circumcision and the cross (5:11; 3:1; 6:14). His parting shot is an ironical jibe at the advocates of circumcision (5:12).

*Discuss how Paul's 'humanity' is expressed throughout the epistle.*

# 3

# From slavery to service
# Gal 5:13–6:10

## (a) Gal 5:13-15. Exhortation to mutual service

The insistence which Paul has placed on the idea of christian freedom could be misleading. It is even possible that there were in the Galatian communities, as at Corinth, certain groups who gave freedom from the law as an excuse for all kinds of laxity. In this second main part of his letter Paul shows quite clearly that christian freedom is not licence but a new kind of service, and that exemption from the law, far from being an open cheque for all kinds of loose living, means in fact *freedom from sin*. For has he not shown in the first part how the law is at the service of sin?

Paul has already mentioned the cardinal virtue of love in 5:6. He now states that the whole law is fulfilled in love of the neighbour (5:14). It is interesting to notice that Paul uses the word 'fulfilled' in this context and not such a term as 'kept' or 'resumed'. In fact it is the love of Christ which Paul sees in his sacrificial death (2:20) undertaken in the fulness of time (4:4). Could it not be that Paul wishes to intimate that neighbourly love is the continuation of Christ's love (6:2)?

*1. Discuss the whole question of the relationship between christian freedom and licence. In what sense can*

*Galatians be called the* Magna Carta *of christian freedom?*

2. *How is law related to freedom?*

3. *How should the church of today teach the fundamental commandment of love?*

## (b) Gal 5:16–25. Exhortation to walk in the Spirit

At first sight it may seem that Paul's use of 'Spirit' and 'flesh' in this section is different from his use of these terms in the first part of the letter, but this is not so. 5:18–19 show clearly that Paul sees a very close relationship between the law and the works of the flesh. It is the law which is explicitly 'against' them (5:23) and thus, ironically, is their instigation and occasion (3:19). The Spirit, on the contrary, is an entirely positive principle of action (5:23). Paul opposes the '*works* of the flesh' to '*fruit* of the Spirit', the former being the products of purely human activity, the latter the external expression of an interior living principle. This passage contains one of the most eloquent expressions of christian morality to be found in the new testament. In the first part of his letter Paul has shown that the christian life is essentially a life in the Spirit, as opposed to a life according to the flesh or the law. This life is begun by faith and baptism. In the second part he proceeds to insist that to this new life there must correspond a new way of living, a new morality. By faith and baptism the christian has indeed died to the flesh and the law mystically in Christ (2:19), but this death has to be constantly realised by a death to sin (5:24). Christian morality according to Paul springs not from a law, but from the interior impetus of the Spirit by which the christian is led and with which he co-operates.

*1. What relationship does Paul see between the law and the works of the flesh?*

*2. What is the connection between the life of the Spirit and christian morality?*

*3. How does Paul express the need for response to the Spirit on the part of man?*

## (c) Gal 5:26–6:6. Exhortation both to mutual service and attention to self

5:16–25 is effectively a synthesis of the whole of christian morality, apparently inserted between 5:15 and 5:26. In this section (5:26–6:6) Paul continues the train of thought interrupted in 5:16 and gives a series of practical exhortations concerning personal and social responsibilities.

*Discuss Paul's practical sense and his knowledge of human nature expressed in this epistle.*

## (d) Gal 6:7–8. Exhortation to sow in the Spirit

Throughout the letter Paul has insisted on the divine aspect of redemption. Here he emphasises the need for human co-operation, applying a familiar agricultural image to the christian life. The kingdom of God is indeed a matter of an inheritance (5:21), but it also involves a process of sowing and reaping (6:7–8). The whole mystery of divine grace and human co-operation is here in a nutshell.

*Show how the images of sowing and reaping express a profound aspect of the mystery of grace.*

## (e) Gal 6:9–10. Exhortation to universal service

One particular example of this 'sowing in the Spirit' is to do good not only to members of the christian community, but also to all men. This note of universality is strikingly new in an age when the emphasis was on the closed community.

*1. What could Paul mean by 'doing good'?*
*2. Is the universality expressed in this section a random thought or is it intimately connected with the rest of the epistle?*

# 4

# Résumé and conclusion
# Gal 6:11–18

### (a) Gal 6:11. Paul's signature

It is very probable that Paul, like other literary men of his
time, employed a secretary who would have been responsible for the production of the manuscript in its present
form and possibly even for the structure and elaboration
of certain parts of the letter. Here Paul adds his signature
to the document which he has dictated or commissioned.

*Why doesn't the fact that Paul dictated a substantial
part of his letters detract from his authorship or from
their inspired character?*

### (b) Gal 6:12–17. Contrast between Paul and the judaisers

At the end of the letter Paul reverts to its main theme, by
opposing the relation of the judaisers to the gospel, here
epitomised in the 'cross of Christ' (6:12), to his own. Paul
is an instrument of the Spirit, they of the flesh. This term
poignantly evokes the antithesis flesh-Spirit, current
throughout the letter, but it is also a clever allusion to
the rite of circumcision (6:12, 13, 15). At the beginning
of the letter Paul referred to the accusation of self-seeking
levelled against him by the judaisers (1:10). He here suggests that the real self-seekers are the judaisers themselves

who are afraid to undergo persecution, the hallmark of genuine christianity (6:12), whereas he, Paul, is true to the real meaning of the gospel (6:14). The 'marks of Jesus' mentioned in 6:17 doubtless refer to this persecution suffered by Paul in the accomplishment of his apostolate.

The whole letter is summed up in 6:15–16. The redemption achieved by Christ so transcends any other religious structure that it can be called a 'new creation' (6:15; 3:28; 5:6), and the new people of God, the new Israel, is constituted by those who act according to this reality in newness of life (6:16).

*What does the often quoted phrase of 6:14 mean in its correct context?*

## (c) Gal 6:18. Final greeting

Paul ends the letter, as he began, with a greeting. After such developments on the idea of *freedom* in the *Spirit*, it is not difficult to envisage the resonances which the terms 'grace' and 'spirit' would have had in the minds of Paul's first readers.

*Is this greeting a mere literary device?*

# General conclusion

## (a) Message

Once it is situated in its historical context it is easy to see that the problem with which Paul was concerned in the epistle to the Galatians was unique in the history of christianity. Christ, his mother, the first disciples and apostles were of the Jewish race. The church was born in a Jewish environment. It was natural that christianity at this early stage should be confused with judaism, that, in some quarters, it should be regarded as just another Jewish sect. The development of christianity during the first century, that is, during the time when revelation was still being continued, showed that this was not in fact the case. Christianity was seen, in conformity with the mind of Christ himself (Mt 28:19–20), to transcend the rigid bounds of judaism, to be a universal, catholic religion. The council of Jerusalem in 49 and the destruction of the Jewish temple in 70 were significant stages in this development. Galatians is one of its most eloquent witnesses.

## (b) Meaning

To apply the phraseology or the teaching of Galatians superficially to any other historical situation would be to distort its original meaning. No one today would consider observance of the Jewish law as a necessary part of christianity, and few would present their baptismal certificate

as a permit for all kinds of licentiousness. Nevertheless
Galatians has a permanent value and relevance for the
twentieth century. The profound meaning of Galatians is
twofold. Firstly, it is a powerful testimony to the fact that
christianity is not identifiable with any one given culture.
On the contrary, it is capable of assuming all cultures, all
true human values, because it is the religion of God's Son
made *man*. This observation has many implications for an
understanding of the church's missionary activity and her
role in the world. Secondly, Galatians indicates the source
and mainspring of christian morality, that is, the life of
the Spirit or, more precisely, the life of a child of God.
The only law for the christian is the 'law of Christ' (6:2)
who loved men and gave himself for them (2:20). All true
christian morality has its source in, and is inspired by, this
love. Christian freedom is not a *carte blanche* to do what
one wants. It is a commitment to Christ and to the service
of all men in Christ. The criterion of christian action is
the obedience of a child to its Father expressed in the
service of one's neighbour.

1. *What is the relevance of Galatians for the church of
the twentieth century?*
2. *Outline the main themes of the epistle.*

# Romans

*Anthony Walker*

# Introduction

There is general agreement among scripture scholars that the epistle to the Romans is of Pauline authorship, and that it was probably written from Corinth in the year 55 AD, towards the end of his third missionary journey. There is some dispute, however, as to whether the letter was originally addressed to the christian community at Rome exclusively, and there are those who suggest that, from internal evidence, it seems likely that copies of the epistle were sent out to many churches, each slightly adapted by Paul or others so as to contain topical allusions and greetings to prominent members of that particular community, and with only the version destined for Rome surviving in our new testament.

Though interesting enough to the biblical historian, this problem hardly affects our understanding of a letter which, wherever its destination, has been recognised throughout the christian centuries as central to Paul's teaching.

Though not a complete summary of the apostle's understanding of the gospel, it remains nevertheless the fullest statement we have of his own theology. In it, he attempts to systematise and set out in greater detail a problem that he had already dealt with, though less adequately and calmly, in his epistle to the Galatians.

The problem he had grappled with so passionately then was one that was already dividing the christian church, both at Jerusalem itself and wherever the ideas of the 'judaisers' took hold. For they taught that all converts to christianity must accept and abide by the law of Moses —must, in fact, become Jews, though Jews who believed that Jesus had fulfilled but not superseded their religion.

Paul, convinced of the radical newness of the message of Jesus by the experience of his own dramatic conversion from the rigorously legalistic form of judaism practised by his fellow-pharisees, saw this newness denied in the attempt to turn the christian church into a Jewish sect. And he objected, violently.

Instead, he set out to show:

(*a*) that the law, without faith, was powerless to save, and was indeed a hindrance and a curse; and

(*b*) that God's glorious future, though still awaited, had nevertheless arrived in the resurrection of Jesus from the dead, and was available and open to the man of faith.

This assertion in Romans of the absolute priority of faith has had a profound and continuing effect on the subsequent history of the christian church, and has often indeed been at the centre of bitter controversy. We need only mention the names of St Augustine, Martin Luther, John Wesley or Karl Barth to see that this is so.

But the epistle has largely ceased today from being a battleground. Though commentators like Ian Paisley may still see Romans as the condemnation of Romanism, there has for some time been a general recognition that the basic premise that Luther took from Paul's writing, namely, that grace precedes all good works, was sound, and that the popular catholicism of his place and period did indeed assume that the business of buying indulgences and venerating relics was of greater importance than a loving faith in the Lord Jesus.

However, the epistle today poses a much greater problem for thinking christians of whatever denomination. For it, too, makes an assumption that most of us would no longer willingly subscribe to. It assumes—as those who have argued or agreed about it have tended until recently to assume—that all men are called to a real and explicit faith in the God and Father of our Lord Jesus Christ, or at least in the existence of a beneficent deity who demands from them a certain and easily-discovered standard of behaviour. Against such a background, it was easy and inevitable to assert that the atheist, the agnostic and anyone who flouted the accepted moral code was insincere, acting against his own better judgement and, in short, a sinner. He had wilfully rejected, after all, the grace of God, and was in consequence doomed to an eternal damnation.

Such a solution will not do today. Instead, if we are to believe that the grace and love of God are truly universal and openly offered to all, and if at the same time we are to accept the plain fact that only a tiny minority of men and women have ever been able to accept the christian gospel in its fulness, while a growing number find it impossible today to believe in any kind of God, then we must seek to re-interpret Paul's message and try to find, beneath his easy but understandable assumption that the non-believer is simply wicked, the living and saving word of God. This is the problem we must ponder over and discuss, if we are not to reject the epistle to the Romans as merely irrelevant.

## Book list

K. Barth, *The Epistle to the Romans*.
C. H. Dodd, *The Epistle of Paul to the Romans*.
M. J. Lagrange, *Épitre aux Romains*.

C. K. Barrett, *A Commentary on the Epistle to the Romans*.

H. Küng, *Justification*.

# 1

## Gentile and Jew
## Rom 1:1–4:25

**Rom 1:1–7. The address**

Paul introduces both himself and his subject-matter to his readers by expanding the typical Greek formula for the start of a letter, which was simply 'A to B, greeting'.

He begins by describing more fully his own position, and goes on to justify his claim to teach his fellow-christians. Using a semitic metaphor, he describes himself as Christ's slave, a common Pauline and indeed new testament term for the follower of Jesus, the ordinary christian. Then he speaks of himself as someone who has been especially called and set apart, like the prophets of old, to be an apostle.

He feels he must insist, as he so often had to insist, that he, who was never a disciple of the Lord while Jesus walked on earth, can nevertheless claim to be a genuine apostle with an authentic commission to preach the gospel. He is an apostle because, though late in time, he nevertheless encountered the risen Lord on the Damascus road, and also because he was sent out to proclaim the good news, not by any church group or christian leader, but by the resurrected Christ.

And what is the subject-matter of his preaching? In verses 3 and 4 he summarises his gospel, making use, it appears, of a well-known christian formula, though adapting it slightly. The formula itself stated that Jesus was born a son of David in the flesh, but was appointed the son of God in the spirit.

This is an existential formula, as used by Paul. In other words, he uses it, not to describe what Jesus is, but the significance of his life, death and resurrection. He was born, that is to say, a real man, a member of our race and a sharer in its weakness, open like us to temptation, suffering and death, but he was raised from the dead as a new kind of man, one who was now with God and so beyond the grasp of such evils.

Paul clarifies this statement by adding to the older formula the assertion that Jesus became son of God in power—that is, was able to manifest and to exercise, as a human being, his divine sonship—only when the spirit of holiness (probably the Holy Spirit, to whom Paul often attributes the work of resurrection) raised him from the dead.

Paul ends his address by slightly altering a conventional Greek word of greeting, changing it to 'grace', which signifies God's gift of salvation, coming to man supremely in Jesus, who is grace incarnate. And then he adds the typically Jewish greeting of 'shalom' or peace, for it is Jesus, the grace of God, who reconciles us with the Father and with each other and thus brings to us a peace we do not deserve and cannot understand.

## Rom 1:8–17. The purpose of Paul's visit explained

Paul begins in verse 8 by giving thanks for the faith of the christians in Rome, and goes on to inform them of his proposed visit. He intends to preach the good news to them, something he has never done before in their community. Yet why, if they already believe, should they need this further proclamation? And why should he be so eager to visit them for this purpose?

He explains in verses 11 and 12. He comes in order to encourage them, and at the same time to find encouragement himself. Thus his task of preaching will strengthen the faith of all, including himself. And that strengthening process will itself be a gift of God in which they will all share.

Notice, too, how in verse 9 Paul describes his work of preaching as an act of worship, a spiritual offering to God the Father.

Finally, the theme of the epistle is re-stated (1:16–17), but this time more precisely. Paul is going to demonstrate to Jew and gentile alike that men are only saved from complete separation from God and from each other, in other words, from everlasting death, by their faith.

And how does faith come about? By the power, or Spirit, of God working through the preacher as he proclaims the good news. For the Spirit provokes and strengthens the faith of both the preacher and his hearers when the gospel is proclaimed.

## Rom 1:18–32. The wrath of God towards the pagans

Paul conceives of God's anger almost as an impersonal force that must fall inevitably upon the evil-doer, and in this case upon the pagan who worships idols and indulges in immorality.

Because this and the next passage, dealing with God's anger towards the Jews themselves, seem to take little account of the mercy of a deity who is elsewhere said to love sinners, or of the predicament of a person who cannot in conscience believe in Paul's God, we may be tempted to skim over it and claim it to be a mere aside and not an integral part of the message of Romans. Yet this would be an error, for it is clear exegetically that the passages in question are by no means digressions.

To understand them, we should instead try to understand their background. To Paul, as to most Jews and many gentiles of his day, it was inconceivable that anyone could fail to believe in the one true God, no matter how shadowy and blurred that belief might be. Yet this God, whose existence was inescapably obvious to all, made certain claims upon his followers. He demanded of them a particular way of life that, again, any man of good will could easily discern.

Those who failed to worship the one God, therefore, and turned instead to idols, and likewise those who lived corrupt and depraved lives, had deliberately rejected a deity in whom, deep down, they believed.

What Paul is saying, therefore, is this. Those who deliberately reject God by devoting their lives to perversity in defiance of what they know to be right will come up against the all-consuming wrath of God. Not only that, but his wrath is already upon them. For their corrupted state itself shows them to be separated from him. Their condemnation to eternal death has thus begun.

*1. Is it obvious in our assemblies that the preacher is sharing a gift with his brethren, and not merely talking at (or down to) them? How could the ministry of the word become more of a mutual enterprise?*

*2. Can one distinguish between preaching that is genuinely an exercise of the powerful Spirit of God and thus creative of faith, and preaching that is not?*

*3. Does mainstream christianity pay sufficient attention to Paul's assertion that Jesus only became fully God's son at his resurrection? Can such a statement be squared*

*with the orthodox doctrine that Jesus, as God incarnate,*
*was always divine? Or doesn't it matter?*

*4. Is it possible to reconcile Paul's teaching on the*
*anger of God towards sinners and non-believers with the*
*assertion that all who follow their conscience will be*
*saved?*

## Rom 2:1–11. God's judgement and man's

Adopting the 'diatribe' style of the philosophers and
preachers, Paul addresses a fictitious person who may be
Jew or gentile but whom one must imagine as raising
objections which the apostle has to counter one by one.

Paul appears at first to be condemning the good Jew or
pagan for doing exactly what he himself has just done—
for declaring that the dissipated life of the evil-doer proclaims that he has been condemned by God already.
Verse 3, however, shows that he is thinking here of the
hypocrite, the sinful man who dares to judge others when
his own life is evil.

Not that Paul means to accuse the law-abiding Jew or
the good pagan who may be doing the judging of the same
kind of loose-living as the man he judges. Instead, he
means to assert that all men are sinners, and so all come
under the judgement of God, whose right alone it is to
judge human beings. To attempt to do so on one's own
behalf is therefore to usurp a divine prerogative.

In verse 5, Paul challenges the cosy Jewish assumption
that the man who enjoys a pleasant life—in this case, a
life free from the dissipations of the wicked pagan—is
beloved of God. Not so, says Paul. The Jew, too, must
recognise the sin in his own life and turn away from it if
he is not also to be condemned.

In verses 9–11, he challenges the further assumption

that, on the day of judgement, God will vindicate his own
chosen people, and his anger will fall solely on the gentiles. God has no favourites, Paul declares, and though he
may seem to contradict this by saying that blessings will
fall upon the Jews first, and then upon the gentiles or
'Greeks', he has already prefaced this by saying that
punishment will also fall first on Jew, then on gentile.

Here we may remark that the day of judgement, or day
of the Lord, was popularly held to be a time when God
would show to the world that the Jews were his chosen
ones by setting them above the nations. It did not signify
the end of the world, nor were the pains and blessings
that would be meted out concerned with the next life,
but with this. Indeed, those times in Jewish history when
they seemed to be triumphant over their enemies, or
when, through their own wickedness, God allowed their
enemies to triumph over them, came to be known, in
their turn, as days of judgement, days of the Lord.

For Paul, however, God's judgement had come de-
cisively into the world when he vindicated the dead Jesus
by raising him to glory, triumphant over all his enemies.
The christian shares in this judgement, this triumph,
when he follows in the way of Jesus. When he sins, however, he is condemned by God as an enemy of Jesus, and
one who deserves not life, but death. Ultimately, though
in ways that are not clear, this judging action of God's
will reach its completion, and the good will be 'sentenced'
to share in the risen glory of their Lord fully and forever,
freed like him from corruption.

## Rom 2:12–16. The function of conscience

The Hellenistic Jews, of whom Paul was one, had taken
from the stoics the idea of the 'natural law', or a fixed code

of morality that could be discovered by any man of good will. For the Jew, this was the law of Moses that God had revealed to them alone, and for the gentile it was those parts of that law that his reason had managed to make out.

The stoics saw conscience as the judgement a man made on his own actions when he found them remiss. It was his accuser. Paul, however, sees conscience as above all a witness that speaks up in one's defence before God, since it is one's judgement on oneself, proclaiming that one has indeed lived up to one's own standards.

Conscience, Paul insists, tells us to follow the law as it has been disclosed to us—if we are Jews by revelation, if we are gentiles by our reason. If we do so, then we do well and escape the condemnation of a God who is judging the world through Christ. But, Paul reminds us, God judges not merely our external actions, but even the secrets of our lives, our hidden thoughts and attitudes.

## Rom 2:17–29. The position of the Jews

In this section, Paul seems to have re-thought what he has already said about the place of the Jew before God. He has declared that God has no favourites: yet his instincts— one might even say his very Jewishness—have made him seem to put the Jew in the front rank: when it comes to the handing out of punishments, it is true, but also when it comes to the handing out of blessings.

Now, he re-states this idea in another way. Yes, he says, the Jews *are* God's favourites. But the real Jews are all those who keep God's law, insofar as they apprehend it. These are the secret, the 'anonymous' Jews, who may or may not be circumcised. On the other hand, the man who is a Jew by birth and circumcision but who fails to keep the law is in fact no Jew at all, and has lost the favour of God.

Paul is often embarrassed and seems to be hedging when confronted with this problem. But whenever he seems to be triumphalist in claiming a privileged position for the Jew, we must keep in mind this clear statement that, at the end of the day, one's membership of the Jewish race is strictly irrelevant.

Here Paul seems to be anticipating the modern notion of the 'anonymous christian', whereby it is claimed, as an antidote to the exclusivism of the churches, that all men of good will, all who follow their consciences, are in fact christians and members of Christ's church, though they may not know it.

*1. What attitude, according to Romans, ought a christian to adopt with regard to those who fail to live according to his own standards of behaviour? Are they to be considered as downright wicked, or simply stupid, or in fact as good people who are following their consciences? How do we avoid judging them?*

*2. Since christians themselves disagree and are uncertain over many major moral questions (eg warfare, population control), can we still speak of a natural law known to men of reason and reinforced and filled out by the law of Moses and the clear teachings of Jesus?*

*3. Paul speaks of the future fulfilment of God's plan in the picture, common to Jewish folk-lore, of a day of judgement. Can we find a more relevant metaphor for the reality that underlies this picture?*

*4. If we follow our conscience, we shall find favour with God. What is conscience? How, in fact, do we follow it?*

*5. Is it really a renunciation of privilege to claim that all good men are truly Jews, or christians, or indeed members of a group to which we belong and which we claim has been especially chosen by God? Has the christian or the Jew any privileges over his fellows?*

## Rom 3:1–8. The privileges of the Jews

Paul reverts both to the diatribe style and to the nagging question of the place of the Jews in God's plan of salvation. They are first of all a privileged people, he says, because God chose them by revealing his message to them before everyone else. Not that they were better than anyone else, Paul hastily adds. They were frequently unfaithful to God. Yet he was nevertheless always faithful to them. He never deserted them. He remained their Lord.

By now, Paul has forgotten about his second point. Instead, he concerns himself with answering the imaginary —and to us rather tortuous—objection that, because the sinfulness of the Jews showed up the faithfulness of God, therefore sin is good. This is not true, says Paul, and in verse 8 we see why he has laboured the point. It appears that, because of his teaching that the follower of Jesus is free from the law, some took this to mean that the christian was free to do what he liked, even to sin. We find this mistake being made by some of the church in Corinth— see 1 Corinthians.

## Rom 3:9–20. All men are sinners, Jew or Gentile

Paul now makes use of a whole string of old testament quotations (verses 11–18) to prove that all men sin. In other words, the law itself (and by law he means the whole of the old testament) proclaims that we all break the law. Thus the law alone is powerless to save us, to prevent our sinning, to pardon us or reconcile us with our God. All it can do is to remind us of our guilt. And since the Jew knows the law more clearly than the pagan, be he never so right-minded, he is hence more actually aware of his own wickedness. This is his second (doubtful) privilege.

## Rom 3:21–31. God reveals his righteousness

God's righteousness, or justice, is shown by his actually justifying or making men righteous, by vindicating and proclaiming them as his chosen ones.

If we accept this action of his in faith, and act accordingly, then we too are made righteous or just; we are reconciled with God, pardoned and at peace.

God revealed his righteousness in the law (again meaning the old testament as a whole). Yet Paul has shown that, in fact, this revelation failed to justify, to vindicate, to reconcile or to save anybody, since all are sinners. It only pointed up man's wretched state.

But now, Paul goes on, in the turning point to his epistle, God has further revealed his justice, but this time outside the old judaism and in Jesus Christ. In him, all men can find their reconciliation and peace. In him, all can escape the anger of God and the condemnation to death.

Paul goes on to explain this statement—though briefly, as it is to be a recurring theme of the epistle. All men have sinned, and therefore all men have deprived themselves of the future blessedness God intends for them, their participation in his 'glory' or richness of being. But God now makes them deserving of this non-corruptible life in a gift of his own free giving—in Jesus Christ, who is grace, the gift of reconciliation in human form.

And Jesus redeems us—he buys us out of our slavery to sin and death—by becoming, in his own death, our sacrifice of reconciliation. Hence we, who deserve to feel God's just anger, find instead his mercy and forgiveness, because we believe.

Paul goes on in verse 25 to explain how this is so. He refers, it seems, to the ark of the covenant, and to the ceremony on the day of atonement when the high priest sprinkled its lid as token of God's forgiveness for his people. Jesus is, in other words, the true 'mercy seat' or cover to the ark, the one who really does make men one with the Father. And it is precisely because he was to come and perform this reconciling work that God refused to deal with those who lived before Christ as their sins deserved, just as now he makes all believers in Jesus righteous and just. In both cases, he displays his own justice and righteousness. To summarise—an active faith in the good news of Jesus' sacrificial death averts God's anger from us and makes us just and righteous.

Paul sums up the passage by declaring again, and more unequivocally than ever, that it is this living and active faith in Jesus that saves all men, not the law. He adds, however, that this does not invalidate the law. The old testament is part of God's plan and reveals something of his loving purposes. Instead, the old testament is fulfilled and given worth by Jesus, since he shows what the law and prophets were getting at and pointing towards.

And Paul begins, in the next chapter, to give some examples.

*1. Does christianity in fact seem to encourage a permissive or a repressive form of society? What kind of society ought it to promote, according to Romans?*

*2. Paul's preaching on freedom seems to have led, in some quarters, to moral laxity. Does this justify the fears some christians feel over terms like 'christian freedom' or 'freedom of conscience'?*

3. *If, as Paul claims, human beings are justified by faith, and yet even the pagans who try to live well find favour with God by their good works, how are non-christians justified today?*

4. *Is salvation more readily available to the christian than to the non--believer? Does God favour, in other words, one minority (and mainly white) group in favour of the vast (mainly non-white) majority of the human race? If he doesn't, then what is the point of being a christian?*

5. *Judaism finds its fulfilment in Jesus. Can this be said also of other non-christian religions? If not, what was so special and distinctive about the revelation made to the Jews?*

## Rom 4:1–8. Abraham, the man of faith

Adopting again the diatribe style, Paul turns to the old testament example of Abraham, claimed by the Jews as their forefather because of his great faith. Although Paul has argued, in the last chapter, that Christ has fulfilled the law, he is concerned now to show that this does not mean he has ratified the legalistic religion of the Jews. Paul is intent upon showing, therefore, the real nature of the old testament religion as based not on legalism, but on faith.

For the Jew, Abraham's faith was a 'work'. That is to say, God rewarded him for something he had done, made him father of the chosen people because he deserved it by his faith.

This, says Paul, is false. After all, he has already shown from the scriptures that all men are sinners, that none keep the law. Now, he goes on, if men are to claim God's favour as their right, due to them for their keeping of the law, then clearly no men can be justified or found worthy of that favour, not even Abraham himself.

But if, on the other hand, justification is a matter of God giving his favour freely to men, not because they deserve it, but as his grace, not their due, then justification comes to men simply because they believe and not for what they do. Law-keeping alone makes no claims upon God.

## Rom 4:9–12. Abraham father of the gentiles

Having repeated his claim that, contrary to Jewish opinion, the law cannot justify anyone, Paul goes on to show that, in fact, Abraham was justified by an act of faith before the law as such existed, and indeed before he had been circumcised or initiated into the religion of Yahweh. That came later, according to the narrative in Genesis. Thus Abraham is the forerunner of the faithful gentile as well as of the faithful Jew.

Abraham's example tells the gentile that all men who believe in God's promises are justified. It tells the Jew that it is not his circumcision according to law, nor his keeping of that law, that finds favour with Yahweh, but his faith.

## Rom 4:13–17. The doom of the law

It must be remembered that, for Paul, faith is more than mere intellectual assent. It is the complete giving of one-self to God in utter trust and confidence. It involves, as he has already stressed, a moral life.

Nevertheless, the promise given to Abraham that he should be the father of God's people was made, not for his keeping of the law, but because he did the right thing—

he believed in Yahweh. Indeed, Paul adds, if keeping the
law had been the pre-requisite, then his faith would have
been pointless. But, he adds in verse 15, all that the law
does in fact is to promise us punishment. It dooms us to
eternal death, since it shows us how we ought to behave
without giving us the power to do so. Moral standards are
important, in other words, but because we are sinners we
cannot keep them. And, because we cannot keep them,
we deserve death. And such would be our lot unless God
freely offered his pardon and life to those who would
accept it.

For God is man's saviour. He raises the dead and
rescues us from death-like situations.

## Rom 4:18–25. Abraham, man of hope

Abraham and Sarah were in a death-like situation—both
old, and she barren. Only Yahweh, said the rabbis, could
unlock the womb and raise the dead. He can bring forth
life out of nothingness.

Without taking account of Abraham's works, God
instead 'counts' or 'considers' his faith, his trust in God's
promise when all seemed so hopeless for him. Though
Abraham could do nothing to deserve God's favour, yet
God 'counts' his faith as though that really merited his
loving attention. He 'pretends' that it is enough, and so
gives the aged couple the promised child.

If we, too, believe and trust in him, not because of our
own good deeds, but because he raised Jesus from the
dead, then he will raise us out of the death our sins
deserve. We are justified, verse 25 tells us, not by the
death of Jesus alone, but equally by his being raised by
his Father from the dead. The Lord's saving work resides
both in his dying *and* his exaltation.

*1. What can Abraham's example add to the commonly accepted notion of the person who 'has the faith' or 'keeps the faith'?*

*2. The 'works' of liturgy and the loving service of our neighbour cannot justify us without the kind of faith Paul describes. Are they, therefore, to be discounted? What is their proper place in the christian scheme of things?*

*3. What of the generous, open, loving, self-sacrificing non-christian? Do his 'works' find favour with God and pardon for himself, even though he lacks faith? Or is faith not required of him?*

*4. Why should legalism be so attractive to many christians? Is it present in official christianity and, if so, how could it be eradicated?*

*5. Paul asserts the saving value of Christ's resurrection equally with his death. Does this need to be re-asserted in modern christianity and, if so, how?*

# 2

# Law and Spirit
# Rom 5:1–8:39

**Rom 5:1–11. From justification to salvation to glory**

For three-and-a-half chapters, Paul has been dealing with the problem of justification. He has shown that, through our faith in the death and resurrection of Jesus, God passes a favourable sentence upon us. We are reconciled with him, and judged to be in the right, or righteous.

This past action has a present effect—we are now in a state of grace. That is to say, we remain reconciled to God because he freely wills it to be so. More than that, our present state enables us to look forward to a future when we shall share God's glory, as Jesus shares it through his rising from the dead.

In verses 3 to 5, Paul goes on to treat of suffering and hope. He believed, as a Jew, that the last times, the final stage in the world's history, would be marked by the persecution of God's people. Therefore the sufferings that christians were being called upon to endure were signs to them that, in Jesus, these last times had truly come. Thus the christian could learn to put up with his trials in the certain hope that they would end in glory.

Hope, for Paul, was more than a mere wish or desire. It meant having confidence in God's promises. But it meant something more.

Hope arises in our hearts because the love of God has been poured out into them, and because the Spirit has been given us. If we remember how, in Ac 2:18 and 33, the same Spirit was said to have been poured out at Pentecost as Joel had prophesied (2:28), we can see that the love and the Spirit of God are one and the same. The Spirit is love, and this love resides within us—not fully, not so as to exclude all wrong or selfish love, but as a pledge, a part-payment of the full gift that is to come.

That is the deeper meaning of hope. It is a pledge. It stands for the partial gift of the Holy Spirit that is ours here and now because we believe, and is a pledge to us that the God who loves us destines us for a glorious future.

In verses 6 to 11, Paul goes on to claim that Christ's death for sinners proves God's love for them. Therefore, he concludes, Christ cannot now abandon us. Having reconciled us, he must go on to complete the rescue operation. Indeed, Paul makes a parallelism here. We were reconciled by the death, we are saved by the life. That is to say, he speaks of the crucifixion in sacrificial terms as that which wins our atonement with the Father, and of the resurrection as that which wins for us new life. Already we can detect a pattern in Paul's thought on the redemptive work of Jesus. By his death, our sinful state as enemies of God is somehow done to death. We escape the angry sentence of everlasting death. By his resurrection, we rise to a new status—we become friends of God by the free gift of the Spirit of his love that dwells within us, leading to glory.

## Rom 5:12–21. Jesus, the second Adam

There was much Jewish speculation at this time about the person of the biblical Adam. Some even spoke of a

heavenly Adam, upon whom God had modelled the
earthly version in the beginning.

Paul takes hold of this trend of thought and re-
interprets it. Without questioning the existence of a first
Adam, he states that it was through this man that sin and
death entered the world. Adam disobeyed God's commandment just as, since Moses, the Jews have disobeyed
the commandments. And what of the time in between,
when there was no law? Forgetting his earlier argument
that all men can discover this law, Paul skirts over the
difficulty by simply asserting that sin existed even then.

For without sin there would have been no death. Here
we may take physical death as a symbol of theological
death. For Paul, bodily death illustrates the consequences
of sin. It isolates a man, cutting him off from his God and
his fellows.

But Jesus, the second Adam, rescues us from this fate.
He wins us the free gift of being reconciled to God and
receiving his loving Spirit into our hearts as the beginnings of a new and everlasting life. From verse 15 to
21, Paul contrasts the work of the first Adam with that of
the second, showing in every instance that the salvation
won by Jesus far outweighs the evil wrought by Adam.
Adam bequeathed to us a life of sin, and one destined to
end in theological death. Jesus, the second Adam, be-
queaths to us a share in his own life of glory. This is the
free gift of grace, the gift that reconciles us to the Father
and justifies us before him so that, however sin may seem
to flourish in the world, this grace that comes to us
through the death and resurrection of Jesus abounds even
more.

*1. The christian, says Paul, should endure persecution
patiently, as a sign that the end is near. Does this mean we*

should not protest against injustices or seek to renew society?

2. *The Spirit is the love of God that justifies and saves all men in Christ. How do we detect, in human love, the presence of the Spirit? Are all who genuinely love thereby justified?*

3. *What meaning can we give to the term 'sanctifying grace'?*

4. *Living in a society where sacrifice was a normal way of expressing devotion, Paul naturally uses this as a metaphor to describe the death of Jesus. Is it a valid metaphor today? Can we be satisfied with saying that God proved his love for us by demanding that Jesus offer himself up to his Father in sacrifice? Or could we express it otherwise?*

5. *Again, what of the metaphor of resurrection? Paul speaks of the exaltation of Jesus as a rising up from the grave, like a person getting up out of bed in the morning. What truth, do you think, underlies the metaphor? What was the resurrection of Jesus?*

## Rom 6:1–11. Baptism as death and resurrection

Paul deals with two problems in this section. First, in a diatribe-style question-and-answer sequence (verses 1 and 2) he repeats his teaching that, simply because God justifies us freely, and independently of our own good deeds, this does not mean that we are therefore free to do as we like, adding his condemnation of the strange idea, apparently to be met with in his day, that we ought to sin so as to give God more scope for exercising his graciousness towards us. Then, in verses 3 to 11, he goes on to explain the true meaning of baptism as a reinforcement of his argument.

The plunge into water that expresses in ritual form a man's conversion, his coming to an explicit faith in Jesus has, despite its strongly semitic symbolism, close affinities with the initiation rites of the mystery religions.

To the Jew, baptism signified a ritual repetition of the plunge of the Hebrews into the Red Sea, where they died to their old life of Egyptian slavery and rose to a new life as the people of God, on its passover journey to the promised land. To the christian, it signifies our participation in the passover of Jesus, his exodus out of this world and from his own condition as a slave to temptation and death, to his exaltation at the Father's side, where he is now fully at one with God and with us by the power of the Spirit that glorifies him. And we should notice how, in verse 3, Paul reminds a community he did not himself evangelise that the fact of our baptismal participation in Christ's death and resurrection was an accepted part of christian doctrine.

It was a doctrine, however, that was in danger of being misunderstood, particularly by converts from paganism. For it could so easily become confused with the initiation rites of the mysteries, in which it was held that the rite itself guaranteed one's sharing in the god's humiliation and exaltation automatically, with no further effort on one's own part. One died with the god and rose with him, and that so effectively that one came from the ceremony as a new man, one who was already living in glory (though a glory that was as yet secret and hidden).

Paul states, however, that it is otherwise with christian baptism. True, it represents in ritual form a sharing in the death and resurrection of Jesus—but only as a commitment. It expresses the fact that, through faith, one has begun to deny the demands of the life of the old Adam, a life dedicated to sin and destined for death. And one has

begun to live with the life of the new Adam, as though
already risen from the dead.

## Rom 6:12–14. The resurrection–life

The christian's escape from the slavery of sin is not over
as quickly as was that of the Hebrews from their slavery to
Egypt. Our release from bondage has only begun with
conversion, faith and baptism. Now it must be lived out,
deepened and intensified. At the same time, however,
resurrection-life is not simply something that will come
upon us in the hereafter, though it will only reach its
fulness then. We must, says Paul, strive to throw off the
shackles of sin precisely because we are already living by
grace, and not merely by law.

We are living already, that is to say, by the risen life of
the new and glorious Adam. We share his loving relationship with his Father and with his brethren, humankind.
And the more we die to self-love, the more do we intensify
this relationship of love, this presence within us of the
Spirit of the glorified Christ. In grace, our resurrection
has begun, and it too will end in glory. And that is something law alone could never win for us.

## Rom 6:15–23. Slaves of grace

In these verses, Paul points up the contrast between the
bondage to the Egypt of sin out of which Jesus called us
when we were baptised into the christian community, the
new people of God. Now, he continues, we are, in a sense,
slaves to righteousness. And by 'righteousness' he means
the action of a righteous God towards those who have
faith in the gospel, the action of making them righteous
by forgiving their sins and pouring his Holy Spirit into

their hearts as a new kind of life that is at odds with their old life, dedicated to sin and death.

It is this Spirit that we must obey if we are to share in God's free gift of eternal life. It is this relationship of love that we must live out and express in our own lives if we are to arrive at the promised goal, the communion of saints. For sin, the opposite to any genuine love for God and men, will only lead to a well-deserved state of death, the final rupturing, that is to say, of any satisfactory relationship with our Father and the human race.

*1. Is there any difference between what Paul claimed to be the common christian teaching on baptism and the sacrament as understood and administered today?*

*2. How do we avoid the trap of turning christianity into a mystery religion, with baptism the automatically-effective initiation ceremony bestowing the Spirit of the exalted Lord as a kind of sacred and saving magic fluence?*

*3. Is baptism necessary as the expression of a christian's conversion to the gospel and his new-found faith in Christ? What does it add to the conversion process?*

*4. Does baptism express any reality to be found in the lives of non-christian men and women of good will? Or is it meant solely to give some kind of advantage to the christian, even from his infancy, over his non-baptised neighbour?*

*5. To be a 'slave' to the demands of the Spirit means to be a 'slave' to the demands of the community. What are those demands today? Are they being met in any obvious way by the baptised? And are the baptised, as explicitly 'the people of God', showing an example of the right kind of fellowship to the wider community in which they are set?*

## Rom 7:1–6. Freedom from law

An axiom of Jewish law stated that one escaped one's legal obligations only at death. And it is this axiom that Paul makes use of here in order to explain how christians are freed from the law of Moses.

He makes an analogy, taking as his starting-point the idea, apparently his own, that the husband in a marriage personifies the law to his wife in such a way that, when he dies, she is freed from her legal obligations as his wife. She need no longer obey her law.

Now, says Paul, Jewish christians were once married, as it were, to the law. They had to obey it, as wife obeys husband. However, they have since become a part of Christ. They form one body with him, since they share his life. But that body has already died, on the cross, and risen again to a new life which is not bound by the prescriptions of the Jewish law.

What is the result? Christians are now the brides of a new husband, who is Jesus, and he makes them give birth to the things of God his Father, whereas their old husband, the law, made them give birth to death. That is to say, by striving to obey Jesus, they enter into a new and loving relationship with God while, in striving to obey the law, they sinned and incurred God's wrath.

Christians no longer serve a written law, but the new law that is the Holy Spirit, dwelling in their hearts.

## Rom 7:7–13. The law and sin

Once more afraid that he may have presented the law in too harsh a light as though it were somehow evil in itself, Paul now takes some pains to prove that the law is in fact holy and good. It seems that the apostle has in mind here both the story of Adam's fall as related in Genesis, and also his own experience of conversion and christian living.

Sin, as the serpent, existed in the Garden of Eden before God had commanded Adam not to eat. But the command brought sin to light, and made Adam's temptation and fall possible. It awakened in him the desire for what was now forbidden fruit, and brought upon him the penalty of death. This illustrates the whole function of the law, and of moral codes in general. They bring sin out into the open and show it up for what it is. But what is thus exposed as sinful becomes attractive to men. They desire it, and not the law. Sin may therefore be said to make use of moral laws in order to increase the force of its temptations.

## Rom 7:14–25. The fight within

But why should men be so strongly tempted to do what they know to be wrong? Because, claims Paul, there are two laws within us all, not one. God's commandments are echoed by an evil set of prescriptions that pull us in the opposite direction—away from life and towards death.

Paul's use of the first person here has led some commentators to see this passage as purely autobiographical, and the account of his own inner struggles. Others of an 'evangelical' temper have in the past had to say that he was speaking of a fictional, non-christian 'I', claiming that, for the justified or 'saved' individual, such a struggle is impossible. The better and more widely accepted solution seems to be that Paul is indeed speaking out of his own experience, but is stating a fact that all men, christian or not, who strive to do good also experience. And that is that, although we know how we ought to behave, we have to struggle continually against the temptation to do the very opposite, to follow our own desires as did Adam in the story of the fall.

And our struggles do not always succeed. Our lower nature leads us into sin. We deserve the death to which this lower nature or 'flesh' is striving to dedicate our lives. But Jesus can rescue us from this fate so that, though we continue, in our unspiritual selves, to commit sin, we strive, in our higher nature, our 'spirit', to serve the law which is, for christians, the Spirit of God's love.

*1. How convincing do you find Paul's explanation of the function of moral codes as showing us what sin is and increasing our temptation and our guilt without having the power to rescue us from either?*

*2. Is there any truth in the accusation that today's uncertainty about what is right and wrong itself increases temptation, since we incline, when given the slightest choice, to opt for the easy way out?*

*3. The life-giving law of christians is the indwelling Spirit. Is he a less demanding code than written laws, or do we need both? If so, in what sense can we be said to be free from the law?*

*4. How do we discover, in the face of internal conflict, the perpetual pull towards selfishness and the inadequacy of generalised codes of conduct, what demands the Spirit is making of us personally?*

*5. Does one judge the worth of a particular course of action by the amount of personal discomfort it is going to demand, or by some other criterion?*

## Rom 8:1–12. Spirit of life

The 'therefore' of verse 1 follows on from verse 6 of the previous chapter, where Paul declared us to be free from our slavery to the law and its condemnation. Here he goes on to show why. The principle of life within us, our 'spirit', has been radically altered by our coming to faith. In some way, we now share in the spirit-life of Jesus. And that life is our new law, the principle we must obey if we would find salvation.

How has this change become possible? Because God sent his Son to deal with sin and deprive it of its power. Jesus became a member of our fallen race, a race dedicated to death and final separation from the Father. He took on this fallen nature of ours so that he might feel the full effects of sin without personally betraying his Father's trust. Thus he underwent temptation and suffering and death.

In Jesus, sin found its conqueror. In him, God has already judged and condemned it. It has been defeated, in principle, by a fellow human-being and on our behalf. And now, the demand of the old law, that we should live righteous lives, has become possible—not that sin has been done away with, but that we who strive, by the power of the renewed spirit-life within us, to die to sin are put into a new relationship with God by virtue of this same spirit.

To refuse to live by the life-principle we share with Jesus would be to limit our lives to love of self, to self-interest and self-concern. And this would be to oppose the will of God and incur the penalty of ultimate banishment from the transcendent future to which the Christ-life directs us from within.

Paul goes on to identify this spirit-principle inside us with the Holy Spirit itself—the Spirit of God which is also said to be the Spirit of Christ. Indeed, it is the risen life of Jesus, since he was himself raised to a new and everlasting life by the Father's Spirit. And, since we are already dead with Christ (though, as we have seen, this process of dying, begun formally at baptism, must be undergone continually in reality, not merely once and in rite) we already share this risen life of his. Our own spirit or life-principle is activated now by his Spirit or life-principle. In the Spirit we become a part of Christ—we belong to him. In the Spirit, too, we shall share in his resurrection. As complete, full and integral human beings, with all that state involves, we shall rise above our present limitations to share a glorious future when the Spirit which is love shall possess us completely. Then shall our death and resurrection with the Lord have come to completion.

## Rom 8:12–30. Children of God and heirs to his glory

It is only because we share the Spirit of the risen Lord that we dare, with him, to call out to God as our Father—indeed, as our 'Daddy', since 'Abba' is a daringly intimate term that no non-christian Jew would have dreamt of applying to Yahweh. It is Paul's contention, however, that we have been as it were *adopted* by God as his children, since we share the life of his Son. We have entered into Jesus' own special relationship with the Father.

And God has consequently called us to share his Son's glory. It is our inheritance, though as God's free gift, not our due, as Paul reminds us in verses 28 to 30. But verses 18 to 27 have already stated that this glory is not for men alone. It is a future to which the whole creation tends, a future for which it yearns.

We who live by the Spirit, we whom the Spirit puts into a new relationship with God, have a responsibility towards a universe that is likewise subject to imperfections, limitations, suffering and corruption and death. It is subject, too, one might add, to abuse and exploitation by self-seeking and non-spiritual men. If it is involved in our sin, however, it is also involved in our glory. It relies upon us to use it aright and help it towards the liberation, the future freedom from limitation, for which, like us, it groans.

And we, who hope for that freedom for all the universe, already possess its beginnings, its first-fruits, since we possess the partial gift of the Spirit who is the life and love of the risen Lord.

### Rom 8:31–39. The victory of love

Again reverting to the diatribe style, Paul assures us of our victory. We, who share the Spirit of Christ, have been acquitted by a judge who is now our adoptive Father. For Christ does not act as our prosecutor but our defender and brother before God. Our trials, our sufferings, should not cause us, therefore, to doubt God's love for us. For they represent our own inevitable participation in the dying of Jesus. Through them, we shall find ourselves more and more dead to sin, and more and more alive in the Spirit, because more and more possessed by love, the love of Christ himself in which we draw closer to God and to each other. For Christ displays to us what God's love for us is like; this risen and glorified man testifies to the future God holds out to us as a race. And nothing that exists, not even the cosmic powers that men in Paul's own day took so seriously and found so threatening, can alter that fact. It is we who must, with the rest of creation, draw towards this promised goal by increasing our relationship of love with God our Father and with our brethren and our world, in the Spirit of our elder brother, Jesus Christ.

*1. We are told that the Holy Spirit is love, and we know that love is essentially a relationship of self-giving. Is it possible or helpful, therefore, to describe the Spirit as relationship?*

*2. Is the possibility of a new and saving relationship with God available only after the resurrection, or are there other ways in which Christ could be considered to be the first-born of his brethren?*

*3. Who are Christ's brethren? Nominal christians? All the baptised? Committed christians only? Or those of whatever religion or ideology who try to transcend the limitations of their own self-love? Or everybody?*

*4. The christian, according to Paul, should bring hope and reassurance to all who struggle to liberate man and his world. Where is this needed and how could it be done today?*

*5. The demand that we help and respect a world that needs our aid if it is to find, with us, its liberation, would seem to make christian involvement in politics obligatory. What form and direction might such involvement well take today?*

# 3

# The place of Israel
# Rom 9:1–11:36

### Rom 9:1–5. The importance of Israel

Half way through his epistle, Paul introduces a theme he has already touched upon, but one that is now to occupy him for the next six-and-a-half chapters. It is the question of the position of Israel in God's plan of salvation.

Some have seen this apparent change of subject as due to Paul's patriotism, as though he were about to end the letter and then decided to say all he could in defence of his own people (perhaps, indeed, because, as apostle to the gentiles, he had been accused of neglecting the Jews), while adding all that could be said in defence of Yahweh for his apparently shabby treatment of them.

And yet, both halves of the epistle are in fact concerned with the same truth—God's free choice of some men before others and his justification of those who have faith in him.

Paul begins by assuring us of his genuine distress that his own kith and kin have, in the main, rejected the good news. He wishes (though in a formula that shows he knows his wish is impossible) that he could be cursed for their sakes, if that would do any good. He recounts their former privileges, their being counted as God's people, the glory of Yahweh they saw at the exodus, the covenants he entered into with them, during their passover journey, at Horeb, Moab, Gerizim and Ebal, the law and temple-worship on which, with deeds of love, the rabbis said the world was established, and the promises of future blessedness. Finally, they who are Paul's flesh and blood are also one in flesh and blood with the patriarchs, and with Christ—for which, Paul adds in verse 5, God is to be blessed.

Some would hold that the apostle identifies God with Christ in this doxology, but most commentators agree that such an identification would be both unique in the Pauline writings and also much too explicit an assertion of Christ's divinity for the new testament period.

## Rom 9:6–13. God keeps his promise

Though Israel has fallen away from faith, Paul is at pains to show that God has still kept his promise. He reminds his readers that membership of the people of God is not merely a matter of race. After all, the old testament shows Yahweh selecting from among the Israelites, and often choosing the more unlikely and apparently less-qualified candidate—Isaac instead of Ishmael, Jacob instead of Esau. In the back of his mind may have been the fact of God's choice of himself, a most unlikely candidate indeed, on the Damascus road.

## Rom 9:14–24. God is always just

Paul now has to explain how this treatment can be fair and just. He does so in a way that few find satisfactory, asserting that God chooses some while hardening the hearts of others; that, like a potter with a lump of clay, he can mould us for whatever purpose he pleases; or that he is far more patient with us than our sins deserve. Behind these inadequate statements, however, lies the deeper truth that the grace of God is freely given; it cannot be won as of right. For Paul goes on to remind us that God is no racist; that membership of one particular nation puts no claims on him; that, in fact, the history of the people of God of old led up to the creation of a new people whose existence owes nothing to race at all. In this context the claims of kith and kin are irrelevant.

### Rom 9:25–29. The new people of God foretold in scripture

Paul now shows that the fact of a renewed people of God is a part of the promise to Israel, and was foretold by the prophets. God has not deceived the Jews, in other words.

### Rom 9:30–33. The fall of Israel

Israel stumbled over the rock. Trusting overmuch in its keeping of the law for salvation, the Jews stumbled at the proposition that faith in Jesus justifies. They were scandalised that non-Jews could find favour with God outside the law, and that Jesus should be preached as the seed of Abraham, the child of promise. We find the same treatment of Christ as rock in 1 Peter 2:6 ff, using a similar composite quotation from Isaiah.

*1. Is the idea of a chosen people consistent with the doctrine of God's salvific will—that he sincerely desires the salvation of all mankind?*

*2. Christianity is predominantly a white man's religion, though even then only a minority interest. Does God therefore prefer the white races, or any particular groups among them? How does he escape the charge of racism if, as Paul says, the call to faith is a free gift?*

*3. If the christian church is the new people of God, what is its role in the world? Is it necessary, or could we do without it?*

*4. Many stumble over ecumenism, and the idea that other christians can be as truly called and favoured as the members of their own denomination. How do we help such people? Or should we even try?*

*5. What of the problems of the wider ecumenism? Is there any way in which we could say that buddhists or moslems, humanists or atheists, are called and chosen by God?*

## Rom 10:1–13. God's righteousness and man's

Again, in verses 1 to 4, Paul gives voice to his anguish for his own race, commending the enthusiasm of the Jews for the things of God. Here is the zealous Pharisee speaking. However, Paul adds, they have gone astray because, instead of accepting the righteousness of God by listening to and believing in the good news, they tried to make themselves righteous merely by their keeping of the law. Yet the law has in fact been fulfilled and terminated by Christ, and anyone who believes in him, of whatever race and origin, will be declared just by the Father.

Quoting from Deuteronomy (30:12 ff) Paul goes on to adapt the words attributed to Moses in order to suit his own purposes. Moses may say that those who keep the law will live by it, but the law itself cannot give life. It cannot make us righteous, for righteousness, if it were a person, would tell us that we cannot, of our own effort, bring about our justification. No work of ours could have brought the messiah into the world, nor caused God to raise him from the dead. All this was pure gift.

On the other hand, righteousness is not impossibly far away from us. Once we have heard the word, the preaching of the gospel, all we have to do is to believe, and to testify to that belief. And though Paul says that faith makes us righteous and our testimony will save us, he is not thereby chopping up the saving process into separate compartments. Belief and confession are but two aspects of the one sincere reaction to the good news. And it is this reaction alone that wins our past justification, our present righteous state, and our future salvation.

And what must we believe? That Jesus is Lord: that this man is the Christ, the anointed of God. And how is he Lord? By his rising from the dead, when he was established by the Father as victor over evil and death.

Finally, quoting Isaiah but adding his own reference to the 'Greeks' or gentiles, Paul again stresses that God makes no distinction between the peoples of the earth. But, whereas in 3:22 he claimed that both Jews and Greeks had sinned, he now asserts that either can find righteousness, not through the law, but through faith. And he ends with a quotation from Joel that he applies to the work of preaching the gospel to the non-Jewish world.

## Rom 10:14–21. Israel is without excuse

In an echo of the previous chapter, Paul has again expressed his sorrow over faithless Israel. Now, once more, he accuses her of going against her own scriptures. Selecting appropriate quotations from Isaiah, Ps 19 and Deuteronomy, he demonstrates her blindness.

Faith justifies. Yet faith is only provoked by preaching. And preachers must therefore be sent. Nevertheless, as the prophets of old discovered, most men reject God's word. And today most Jews reject the word of Christ—a message, that is to say, that is proclaimed by his authority and by men whom he has sent.

Israel has heard this message. It was preached first of all, in fact, to the Jewish communities in the empire. Why, then, did it not recognise the gospel as the fulfilment of its law and prophets?

The answer, to Paul, is clear, though his solution may not satisfy us. Israel rejected the gospel out of jealousy. And he quotes Isaiah to back him up. The Jews are jealous over the pagans finding God's favour and being called into the ranks of the new chosen people. So they rebel, as many of them have often done, against the word of Yahweh.

*1. If the law is really a cursed catalogue that merely serves to convict us of sin before the divine tribunal, in what sense is Christ the termination and fulfilment of the law?*

*2. Who today have the authority to preach Christ's word? How do we judge whether individuals have been truly sent on this mission?*

*3. The preaching of the gospel provokes faith in those whom God is calling into the new people of his choice. How far must the gospel message be adapted, however, so as to be more readily heard and understood in different periods and cultures?*

*4. How far is christian preaching today patterned by a white, European, capitalist view of the world and the gospel?*

*5. Does God call everyone into the community of believers? Given adequate preaching by the church and good will on their own part, would all men become christian, save for a few obviously wicked individuals?*

## Rom 11:1–10. The doctrine of the faithful remnant

If Israel is disobedient and faithless, does this mean that God has rejected his own people? No, says Paul, and

points to himself (and, by implication, to all other christian Jews) as living proof to the contrary.

He then cites the story of Elijah as further evidence
that, however rebellious the people as a whole, God has
always preserved a faithful remnant. That remnant today
is christian Jewry—chosen, Paul adds, not because they
were better or more worthy than their fellows, but purely
by the grace of God.

As for the rest of the Jews, Paul can only explain their
failure to respond to the gospel by alleging that God has
deliberately made them unable to believe. Though the
verb in verse 7, '*were not allowed* to see', is in the passive
mood, the quotations from Deuteronomy and Ps 69 that
follow show God acting, or being requested to act, very
positively.

How else could Paul account for the fact that the
majority of his race had failed to accept the good news
about Jesus? If the call to faith and justification is a free
gift of God, then the failure of the Jews to make that act
of faith must somehow be God's doing. And Paul assumes,
furthermore, that not to be called is not to be justified or
saved. This is consistent with his idea that rejection of the
natural law is a sinful act. Yet he is obviously unhappy
with the notion. He appears to be floundering—unable to
credit faith to anything other than the free gift of God,
yet reluctant to think that his own race has been, on the
whole, condemned.

## Rom 11:11–24. God's plan for the Jews

In this section, he goes as far as he can in defence of the
non-christian Jews. Certainly, they have fallen. But their
fall is not final. And it would be wrong for the gentiles to
rejoice over it, since it was because the Jews rejected the

gospel so massively that Paul and his disciples began to preach to the non-Jewish world.

And Paul explains that his own preference for preaching to the gentiles, far from implying that he has himself rejected his own race, is intended rather to make the Jews jealous, to goad them into listening more eagerly to the good news themselves.

He reminds the gentiles, too, that it was the Israelites and not themselves who were first chosen by God. If the christians are the new Israel, it is because they have fulfilled the history of the Israel of old, which was the holy dough that now sanctifies the batch, the cultivated olive stump on which the wild, or gentile, olive branch has been grafted now that the original branch has been broken off for its lack of faith and reliance on works.

The gentiles are not, therefore, chosen because they are better or more worthy than the Jews. On the contrary, just as God has rejected the Jews for their disobedience, so can he equally reject the gentiles for their sins. Meanwhile, if the non-Jew shows faith now, how much greater will be the faith of the Jews, to whom the worship of Yahweh comes almost naturally, when they too come to believe.

## Rom 11:25–32. The completion of God's plan and conversion of the Jews

Paul's christian instinct tells him that God cannot have rejected the Jews in a permanent way. Yet he cannot, at the same time, see how they are at present justified and on the road to salvation, since pardon, justification and salvation come by faith, which is a gift God has denied to the mass of Paul's own race. It must be, therefore, that they will all (or most) be converted at some future date.

## Rom 11:33–36. A hymn to God's glory

Thus Paul can praise God, confident that, however impossible it might be to understand his ways (and, in this case, his dealings with the Jews) yet he is a God who shows his mercy in justifying the most unlikely folk and giving his grace even to pagans in preference to what were his own people. And because faith alone brings with it reconciliation, and yet faith is also an act of God's grace, he alone deserves to be glorified by men. That this is no mere pious ejaculation will become evident in the ensuing chapters.

*1. If only a faithful remnant from among the Jewish people entered the new Israel, it seems that this new Israel is destined itself to be forever a mere remnant of the whole human race. Is this to be regretted, or accepted with equanimity as a part of God's plan?*

*2. What was the function of the remnant in Israel, and what is the function of the christian church today, as remnant? What witness might a remnant church perform when it comes round to accepting its role as remnant?*

*3. The majority of men do not believe in Christ as saviour. Is this because the gospel has not been adequately preached to them? Because they are not destined by God for membership of the new Israel? Because they are evil?*

*4. What of those who have heard the gospel and are fairly familiar with it—Europeans, for example, many of whom have had a christian upbringing and education? Have they been rejected by God? Are they, with the non-christian Jews, condemned to everlasting death? Or can we help Paul out in his efforts at understanding the mystery of the divine call to church membership and the fact that few seem to have received that call?*

5. If non-christians are not, on the whole, deprived of God's grace, how does this square with Paul's teachings in this chapter, and with the whole missionary activity of the church? Do we, in fact, need missionaries, or could they be better employed?

# 4
# Moral questions
# Rom 12:1–16:27

**Rom 12:1–2. Spiritual sacrifices**

Up to this point in the epistle, Paul has been concerned
with dogmatic teaching. Now he turns to look at ethics.
Some commentators in the past have found this shift
awkward, for they felt that the apostle, having just dealt
the death-blow to ideas about the saving value of good
works, was now re-habilitating them. Objections like this
were dictated more by confessional loyalties than by
attention to Paul's thought, however, and it is generally
recognised today that the kind of faith Paul has been talking about all along is an obedient faith (1:5), and one
that is not merely an assent to a series of doctrinal propositions but the giving of our whole being to a God who
justifies us freely and without our first deserving it.

It is this mercy of God's towards us that Paul suggests
should be our motive for right living. He uses technical
words associated with ritual worship like 'offer', 'holy',
'pleasing', to describe such behaviour as a sacrifice, though
of a spiritual kind.

Already the rabbis distinguished between temple sacrifices and an inner or spiritual offering, and already they
claimed the latter to be more important. Indeed, it was
because of this teaching that judaism was able to survive
the destruction of its temple and its whole system of sacri-

fice in 70 AD. Paul agrees about the importance of spiritual
sacrifice—spiritual, not because it is purely interior and
unconnected with outward behaviour, but because it is a
life of obedience to the will of God that is discovered and
dictated to us by our human intelligence. For, according
to stoic philosophers and hellenistic Jews like Paul who
had absorbed much of their thought, the intellect was
man's supreme spiritual faculty. Thus to make use of our
intellect to discover God's will, and then to go ahead and
carry that will out, this is to offer spiritual sacrifice of a
truly acceptable kind.

But this will demand that we live as though Christ were
really risen from the dead and the last times really upon
us. Our intellects have been renewed by this knowledge.
We have come to understand things in a radically
different way. We must now revolutionise our way of
living to accord with this new outlook of ours.

## Rom 12:3–21. Performing the sacrifice

Paul's statement of the revolutionary principle we must
now obey could be summed up in one word—*community*.
Speaking first of the local christian community (12:3–13),
he reminds it that, though made up of many members, it
forms as it were one body with Christ. The 'body'
metaphor is commonly met with in antiquity to describe
a particular group. Here, however, Paul uses the term
only as a simile, whereas he will later be able to say that
christians *are* the body of Christ (eg 1 Cor 12).

We are one with the glorified Lord because we share
his Spirit, his love for God and men. Thus we are united,
in the Spirit, not only to Jesus, but to one another. Sharers
of his risen life, we must make use of the varying gifts the
Spirit brings, not so as to win personal honour or prestige,
but so as to serve the community.

Paul's list of various activities in the Roman church should not be taken as exhaustive, systematic or relating only to the work of particular officials. It does reflect, however, the loose and flexible type of organisation that was to be found in these early churches. It is nevertheless interesting that, as in 1 Cor 12, the prophets are placed first. These were men—or women—who had the ability of applying the gospel to a particular situation, of making the good news relevant, while the preacher explained the christian message in general terms and the teacher probed into it more deeply to work out a theology. We should also note that the administrator is likewise seen as having been endowed by the Spirit for his work of service and worship.

The Spirit of Christ that is in us binds us, if we obey it, to all our fellow christians. But it binds us, too, to all our fellow men. If we learn to forgive, to forgo the taking of revenge, to do good to those who treat us badly, the fellowship of all mankind for which Christ died and the churches exist will finally come about. The last times shall have fully arrived.

*1. Is it sufficiently obvious, from the ritual of the church, that the liturgy exists in order to promote and celebrate the spiritual sacrifices of which Paul speaks? Or does communal worship seem at times to be an end in itself?*

*2. Judaism was well able to survive the destruction of its sacrificial system. Could christianity exist without its sacramental system? Do the sacraments give christians any personal advantage when it comes to their performing of spiritual sacrifices?*

*3. The effectiveness of liturgy is to be judged by the extent to which it encourages spiritual sacrifice. And the*

worth of spiritual sacrifice can be seen by the way in
which christians help create community. How do we set
about this task in our local church?

4. How can we detect the presence of prophets in the
christian church? Why do they seem so often to be at
loggerheads with the administrators? Is not this very
tension destructive of community?

5. The church community exists in order to promote
fellowship throughout the whole human race. In which
areas would you say the church's co-operation in this field
is most urgently needed or most obviously lacking?

## Rom 13:1–7. Obedience to every authority the duty of the christian

It has long been assumed that Paul is merely repeating a
traditional Jewish attitude when he declares rulers and
government officials to have been appointed by God and
as wielding his divine authority. Dr Cullmann, however,
claims otherwise. The 'authorities' mentioned in verse 1
are angelic, not human powers. It is these Paul conceives
of as having been appointed by God to influence and
direct civic rulers. It is to the angelic authorities, Cullmann would say, and not to the magistrates, that the
christian is bound in the first place to submit.

Even if we accept this explanation, however, it is clear
that, in Paul's view, the christian must still respect and
obey human authorities, since they certainly judge and
punish on God's behalf even if their authority is not
strictly divine. Their job, in fact, is to anticipate the final
judgement by bringing down the righteous anger of God
upon the wrongdoer here and now. Hence they are to be
feared only by the wicked, and not by the average church
member.

This may seem an excessively conformist and middle-class attitude, especially when we remember that the letter was written in the days of Nero. But it must be borne in mind that Paul was convinced that the world was soon to come to an end. Until that date, he assumed that Rome would continue to rule. Indeed, if christians were to have the chance of creating any real kind of fellowship in the short space of time left to them, Rome *must* continue to rule. There was no other power to come in and fill the gap.

Stable government must have seemed to Paul a prerequisite for the carrying out by the church of its task. Far from issuing a call to christians generally to protest against social injustices, of which there were many in his day, he may well be rebuking, in this passage, certain members of the community in Rome for doing that very thing!

## Rom 13:8–10. Love as fulfilment of the law

Paul now reminds his readers that it is love for the community that must inform their obedience to the authorities. For he tells them that love is the one thing we owe and ought to owe to our neighbour. If a man truly loves others, he cannot sin: he keeps the law. More than that, he completes it. For love demands much more of him than the law requires. It knows no limits, no bounds. Since it is the Spirit of the risen Jesus himself, it urges us on from within to offer our whole lives in spiritual sacrifice by opening out our hearts to God and the brethren in the manner of Jesus.

Is Paul here introducing a new law that does in fact justify? On the contrary, he is reminding us that the sincerity of our response to the saving mercy of God, his gift of the Spirit, will be shown by the effort we make to keep this law, to live by the Spirit.

## Rom 13:11–14. The time of crisis

It is particularly urgent that we begin here and now to follow the dictates of this inner law. Why? Because the 'hour' or 'time' is already here. The 'world'—that is, society as dedicated to self-love and thereby doomed to death—and the 'flesh'—the individual who is similarly dedicated and doomed—have in principle been judged and condemned already in the death of Jesus. Since his resurrection, a new life has been abroad in the world and at work in the hearts of men to conquer sin and death. We are living in the 'last times', therefore, when that conquest is nearing its completion.

The day of complete victory will soon dawn, a day when sin and death shall be no more, and Christ will be revealed in his risen glory—a glory he will share with his faithful ones. If we are to find ourselves in that number, we must put off like a garment our old way of living and put on, instead, Christ and his way as a suit of armour that will shield us against God's condemnation and wrath.

The metaphor of the taking off and putting on of clothes has led some commentators to see behind this passage an ancient catechism for preparing candidates for baptism, where the taking off of clothes before the baptismal plunge and the putting of them on again afterwards may already have been given the symbolic meaning of the initial rejection of the old life of sin and the beginning of living the new life of grace that is the meaning of the plunge itself.

*1. Despite Paul's teaching on the duty of obeying the directives of the state, we know that, in fact, christians did at times refuse to do so. Indeed, tradition tells us that*

*Paul himself was martyred in Rome for refusing to give up his preaching of the gospel. Was such action therefore wrong?*

*2. Christian churches have often compromised, preferring peaceful co-existence to outright defiance of the state. Are they, in so doing, merely obeying Paul's own injunctions? Are there, in other words, situations when the church ought to compromise? And, by the same token, situations when it ought to protest, come what may?*

*3. We may feel discomforted by statements that only the wicked need fear the arm of the law or that judges wield a God-given authority. Is Paul's apparently unconditional support of the establishment, the* status quo, *justified by his own situation? Can it be explained satisfactorily by appealing to his assumptions about the approaching end of society in its present form? Or was he simply wrong to speak so?*

*4. In what is to many a 'permissive' age, yet an age when the term 'love' is used as the supreme principle and justification for all kinds of human behaviour, can Paul be accused of encouraging laxity by replacing law by love, or is the law of love more demanding than any moral code?*

*5. Paul speaks of an 'age' that began at a definite date, the day of Christ's resurrection, and will end at a definite date, the day of judgement. Can we talk in those terms today, or are there other ways of saying what Paul was trying to express?*

## Rom 14:1–12. The strong who despise the weak, and the weak who condemn the strong

One of the major themes of this epistle is the idea that those who have been justified by faith must live now by the Spirit of love that has been poured into their hearts. That means, as Paul has already stressed, that christians must live in community with one another, without distinction between Jew, for example, and Greek. Here he deals with a further cause for division in the community, the problem of the scrupulous christian who still clings to inherited traditions and outworn customs about diet and feast-days and teetotalism. What exactly these customs were or where they came from is difficult to know with any certainty today, though it is true that some converts from judaism still set great store by the observance of sabbaths and monthly or annual festivals.

Paul cares nothing for such observances in themselves, for they are valueless as far as salvation is concerned. What he does care about is the fact that the disputes they engender are endangering the unity of the christians in Rome. This is the kind of problem, indeed, that he had already met with in the church at Corinth (eg 1 Cor 8:7–11) and was to meet with again with the christians at Colossae (eg Col 2:16–18).

The strong-minded brethren, whom Paul agrees are right, should not however despise the weak for observing these things in all their rigour. Similarly, the weaker christians should resist the temptation of condemning the strong as sinful and lax. Each, in other words, should recognise that the other is following his own conscience, even though, in the case of the weak, that conscience be misguided, and that the actions of either group are therefore acceptable to God.

God does not himself despise the weak for clinging to outmoded regulations, nor does he condemn the strong who have the courage of living without them. Indeed, adds Paul in verse 7, none of us lives and dies alone. Surprisingly, he does not go on to explain that we live and

die always in community, though some commentators and
many preachers have taken the verse in the past as saying
just that. Instead, Paul goes on to remind us that we live
and die in the company of Christ, who has already died
and is now risen so as to become Lord of all men, living and dead. With this in view, Paul quotes Isaiah as he
stresses that our only judge will be the God who claims
us, in Christ, as his own.

## Rom 16:13–23. Scandal and doubt

Although men are free to follow or not to follow the kind
of custom Paul has been speaking about, nevertheless the
weaker christians, though perhaps no longer condemning
their stronger-minded brethren, may become upset by the
latter's free and easy behaviour. Even more, as verse 23
clearly states, they may thereby be led into sin. For, if
they are confused and doubtful about whether or not to
obey some regulation concerning, for example, the eating
of meat, and then go on in fact to disobey, they will be
acting against their own conscience, albeit a misguided
one. They will be doing something that they judge to be
probably wrong. They will be sinning, and that through
the example of one of their fellow christians.

Paul argues therefore for moderation. He does not say
that the strong must follow the customs of the weak in any
permanent way. What he does say is that they ought certainly to do so in those circumstances when they would
otherwise lead their brothers into confusion and sin. In
other words, they must restrict their own freedom of
action when love for the community demands it, for it is
the growth of fellowship and community, not what a man
does or does not eat or drink, that is the kingdom of God
growing amongst us.

*1. The church seems to have been squabbling about its traditions and splitting itself up into quarrelling factions even from apostolic times. What are the main areas of conflict today? How would Paul have us settle them?*

*2. Observances about food or the keeping of holy days seem to be discounted as worthless by Paul. How can we therefore justify the practice of fasting and abstinence, the keeping of the sacred seasons and feast-days of the liturgical calendar, the observance of the christian Sunday?*

*3. Would it be true to say of the church today that the more liberal-minded christians tend to despise their conservative and traditionalist brethren, while the latter often condemn the progressives as self-indulgent, disloyal and a danger to faith and morals? Has Paul a lesson for each faction?*

*4. To follow one's conscience is to do right. What is conscience? Why should it be followed, even when erroneous?*

*5. Why should we take notice of the misguided conscience of a fellow-christian? Why should we not pressurise or cajole him into acting against that misguided conscience? Is there never any situation when we might have to try and prevent another person from following his conscience?*

## Rom 15:1–6. Advice to the strong-minded

Paul continues, in this section, to advise the stronger-minded christians to bear with the foibles of their weaker brethren. He has already asked them to do so for the sake of unity. Now he adds a further reason.

Christ did not simply think of himself while he lived among men. He thought of us in our weakened, sinful state. He acted for us, suffered for us. Paul gives no example from Christ's life, however. Instead, he cites prophecy, quoting Ps 59 in order to show that to put up with other people's weaknesses, though it causes a certain amount of suffering, is a part of God's plan for setting up his kingdom. How can there be love and fellowship without tolerance?

Paul will return to this point in verse 7, widening it out into a general call for unity. First, however, he makes an aside about the importance of scripture (ie the old testament) in general for the christian. The scripture is a message of hope. It tells the story of how God's faithful ones kept on trusting in him despite the apparent hopelessness of their situations. And God did not let them down. But these characters from the old testament prefigure Christ who, even when dying for our weaknesses, never gave up hoping that his Father would come to his aid.

The lesson is clear. After examples like that, surely we should be able to put up with the petty irritations we feel over the fussiness of our more timid brethren? After all, we do not glorify God by bickering or leading others into sin, but by living in community.

## Rom 15:7–13. Expanding the theme

Paul's appeal for fellowship between strong and weak opens out into a general appeal for unity. Christ glorified God by fulfilling the old testament prophecies. And these, Paul reminds his readers, not only foretold a messiah; they also foretold that other nations (which Paul takes to mean the gentiles) shall offer their praises to God and put their hope in him through the same Jesus Christ.

He ends with a prayer that is rich in theological insights. God is the God of hope. He has revealed to us that he is to be trusted absolutely. He who saved Jesus from death can and will carry out his plan for our salvation, despite any appearances to the contrary. As evidence of this, he has already imparted to us a share in Christ's risen life, the Holy Spirit. This gift is the pledge and the beginning of our everlasting life. It is the kingdom amongst us. This fact gives joy and peace to those who believe in God, who hope in him. All will be well; and, if we doubt it, the Spirit can remove those doubts by flooding our hearts with a deeper love and trust in the Father.

### Rom 15:14–33. Paul's work and future plans

Paul now starts to bring his letter to a close in one long epilogue. He begins by explaining what his work consists of, and why he has written for once to a community of christians he did not himself found. He is, he says, a 'priest' of Jesus Christ because, by his preaching, he is able to bring the gentiles to faith in God—to 'offer' them, as it were, in 'sacrifice'. He preaches, what is more, where the gospel message has not yet been heard, since this will hasten on the time when all the world shall, in principle, have heard the good news, and when Christ shall therefore return.

However, he is going to make an exception in the case of the Roman community, since he plans to make for Spain after he has taken back to Jerusalem the collection he has been gathering for the poor christians there, and will call in on the church in Rome on his way. In fact, the collection itself was a sign of unity, rather like the temple tax by which Jews from all over the empire showed their own allegiance. That is why Paul prays it will be accepted by James, the Lord's brother and leader of the Jerusalem church. Paul wishes to demonstrate his own unity with that church, split as it is between those who keep the Jewish law with its prescriptions about food and temple worship, and those who claim that Christ has swept such things aside. Paul, though belonging to the latter or 'strong' party, is taking this collection to James, who is one of the 'weak', as a token of fellowship and love. Indeed, in order to reassure the scrupulous or judaising christians there, Paul will even undertake a fast of purification and take part himself in temple worship, thus living out the lesson of compromise he has been teaching the Romans. What is more, when he does finally come to Rome it will be as a prisoner, since he will be arrested in Jerusalem.

*1. Can the reading of the old testament help christians today? Are there outside the bible other means by which we can read or hear a message of hope from God? Is christianity too bible-centred, or not bible-centred enough?*

*2. Are the churches today communities of joy and peace? Could they express their joy more clearly in their services, their outlook on life, their public image? Do they work actively enough for peace?*

*3. Has the world heard the gospel yet? How has it responded to the good news? What should be the christian minister's first priority—to preach the gospel, or to help create fellowship in the world?*

*4. The christian churches were evidently deeply divided in Paul's own day, none more so than the community in Jerusalem. Were those divisions as deep as the divisions between the churches today? Will the churches ever unite completely? Is it important that they should?*

*5. How would Paul have us work for christian unity? What compromises might the various parties have to make today? What compromises are we ready to make?*

## Rom 16:1–23. Personal greetings, plus a final warning

There are commentators of standing who hold that Paul's letter, as addressed to Rome, ended originally with the final 'Amen' at the end of chapter 15. In this case, they would say, the section we are now dealing with is an addition made by Paul to the version he was sending to the church at Ephesus. They assert, in support of this theory, that the apostle was unlikely to know so many christians by name in a church he had not even visited as yet, and that the Prisca and Aquila of verse 3, though exiled from Rome, settled eventually in Ephesus (see Ac 18). There is no evidence of their returning to Rome.

Whatever its destination, however, the list of names in verses 1 to 16 does contain some interesting information. We read, for example, of a deaconess called Phoebe. Was she a church official, or merely a voluntary worker? The question is in fact inadmissible, since at this stage any precise division between the two functions had probably not been made.

We may note, too, that the church met in the house of Prisca and Aquila (whether in Ephesus or Rome). This reminds us that, though the 'churches' of the mystery gods met in people's houses, their worship was performed in a cult centre, a holy place. The christians, however, knew of no such places. The eucharist, their main act of worship, took place in the family dining-room, and not in any building set especially apart for the purpose.

What of the two apostles, Andronicus and Junias (who was probably a woman)? Had they encountered the risen Christ? That is for Paul the qualification of being an apostle of Jesus. But he also talked of apostles of the church, men sent out by their fellow-christians and not directly by the Lord. Were they rather in this category? We do not know.

The warning in 16:17–20, though suddenly interposed between the list of those who are to receive the letter and those (16:21–23) who join with Paul in sending greetings, seems fairly certainly Pauline. What exactly provoked these second thoughts is again not clear, except that it resulted from the activity of those who set great store on matters of diet. It is their useless regulations about food and not the sin of gluttony Paul is condemning here, and their attempt at convincing their fellow-christians of the need for such rules. Indeed, he condemns such work as at enmity with God's purposes, and seems to foresee difficulties for those who cling to the true gospel, for he reassures them that God will eventually triumph and peace prevail. In the meantime, he prays they will increase in the Spirit of Christ who is grace, love and pardon.

## Rom 16:25–27. The final doxology

Again, some commentators doubt whether this section of praise is Paul's work. Versions of the letter exist that end at chapter 14, and this, they think, may be due to the epistle having been copied out by a heretic called Marcion who disliked the tone of chapters 15 and 16, since he found the type of christianity he was proposing firmly condemned in them. In that case, he could have tagged a doxology of his own devising at the end of 14.

Then christians with the fuller version, finding the original doxology to the version destined for Rome at the end of 15, and that intended for the christians at Ephesus at 16:20, might well have added Marcion's composition to round off the letter more emphatically. In that case, they probably added the identification of the 'mystery' with Jesus (16:25) to make the passage orthodox.

This would accord well with Paul's own view that the plan of God for the salvation of men, becoming progressively clearer in the old testament, has been made known fully in Christ Jesus. This is a mystery, therefore, not meant to be kept secret as the preserve of a privileged few, but to be proclaimed throughout the world—the mystery that man is saved through a real and living faith in the resurrection of Jesus from the dead.

*1. The early church seems to have functioned quite well without any church buildings. What are the purposes of such buildings today? How do such buildings differ from the temples and holy places of other religions?*

*2. If the home is the more traditional place for celebrating the eucharist, would there be any advantage in reverting more widely to that practice today? Why do house celebrations often arouse opposition among christians?*

*3. How do we avoid making a god of customs, habits and rules if these are strictly irrelevant to the living of the christian life today? Can you think of any that might well be discarded?*

*4. Does it matter that some of this epistle may not be the work of Paul himself? Does its value, in other words, rest solely on Paul's authorship, or on some other cause?*

*5. Is Romans relevant to our situation today? How do we hold that faith alone justifies and yet say that the 'mystery' is meant for all men, most of whom do not believe, apparently through no fault of their own?*

# Ephesians

*Duncan Macpherson*

# Introduction

The structure and contents of Ephesians immediately marks it off as a very unusual epistle. Like Colossians it falls into two recognisable parts: a doctrinal section (Chapters 1–3) and a section of moral teaching (Chapters 4–6).

A further breakdown of the structure and contents may be useful as the argument of the epistle is sometimes rather long-drawn out and difficult to follow.

## Doctrinal section: The new brotherhood

1 : 1–3 *Introductory greeting*

1 : 3–14 *Thanksgiving*
Beginning of a highly stylised thanksgiving for the blessings of God in Christ. God has chosen us for these blessings before the world began. The purpose of this choice was twofold; that we should be holy and that we should be sons of God. This choice is a free gift. The same gift by which we are enabled to realise God's plan to sum up everything in Christ. Gentiles now share with Jews in receiving this good news. The 'seal of the spirit' is the guarantee of the future inheritance which both Jews and gentiles are to share.

1 : 15–23 *A prayer for the readers of the epistle*
The writer thanks God for the faith of the readers and

prays that they may understand the hope to which they are called, the glory of their inheritance, and the greatness of God, the giver of this inheritance.

### 2:1–10 *The dead raised*

Thanksgiving resumes. The readers were once dead in sins and wickednesses. Their relationship with God was one of being judged. In mercy and love God gave them life, enabling them to share in the risen exalted life of Christ. They did not deserve this salvation through any good works of their own. Nevertheless one of the results of this salvation is that the redeemed will devote themselves to 'good works'.

### 2:11–22 *Reconciliation of Jew and gentile*

Previously the gentile readers had no share in Israel's covenant with God. Now through the blood of Christ the barrier separating the gentiles from the true Israel has been destroyed. Jews and gentiles are now reconciled as members of the same household.

### 3:1–13 *The place of Paul in God's plan*

The secret that Jews and gentiles were to share equally in the same body of Christ was hidden from earlier generations but has now been revealed to the apostles and prophets. Paul, too, despite his unworthiness has been given the special privilege of proclaiming the good news of Christ to the gentiles. In this way even the principalities and powers are able through the church to learn the wisdom of God as revealed in Christ.

### 3:14–21 *Conclusion of thanksgiving prayer*

Prayer that readers may be given inward and spiritual strength, rooted in love so that they may understand the inexpressible and infinite character of the love of Christ. Writer ends thanksgiving prayer with doxology and amen.

## Section of moral instruction: An appeal to unity

### 4:1-3 *The bond of peace*

The readers should live up to their calling. Unity in the Spirit should be constantly strengthened by their attitudes of gentleness, humility and patience towards each other.

### 4:4-6 *The basis of christian unity*

The unity of christians is seen as stemming from the sevenfold unity of: Spirit; body; hope; Lord; faith; baptism; God and Father.

### 4:7-16 *Using God's gifts for the whole church*

Thus all individual gifts should be used for the building up of unity within the church.

### 4:17-24 *Two differing life styles*

The illumination received in baptism enables the baptised to abandon their pre-christian style of life; sexual immorality is a case in point.

### 4:25-32 *Further contrasts*

The author goes on to enumerate other contrasts of moral outlook which should distinguish christians from pagans.

### 5:1-20 *The basis of christian morality*

The imitation of God and of his love as revealed in Christ should be the basis of all christian morality and christians should behave like children of the light and thus reprove the very different behaviour of the pagans.

### 5:21-33 *Marriage and the love of Christ for the church*

Here the writer gives specific instruction to married couples. Their love for each other and the mutual giving of their sexual union serve as an image for the relationship between Christ and the church.

**6:1–9** *Instruction in child–parent and slave–master relationships*
Common membership of the church gives a new understanding to these social relationships as well.

**6:10–21** *The holy war*
Christians should arm themselves for the struggle with the evil powers who are responsible for the wickedness in the world. Incessant prayer is of vital importance.

**6:21–24** *Personal news and final greeting*
Paul represented as commending Tychicus. A final blessing and prayer.

## Book list

Not many books are currently available on Ephesians but the following may be found useful.
1. Articles on Ephesians in:
    (a) The *New Catholic Commentary* (London 1969).
    (b) The *Jerome Biblical Commentary* (London 1968).
    (c) Peake's *Commentary on the Bible* (London 1962).
2. *The Epistle to the Ephesians* by John Allen in the SCM *Torch* paper-back series is a useful if very elementary commentary.
3. *Ephesians, Baptism and Pentecost* by J. C. Kirby (London 1968) is widely referred to in this commentary. It is not difficult to read and is certainly a most valuable and important study.
4. *Studies in Ephesians*, ed F. C. Cross (London 1956).
5. *The Key to Ephesians* by E. J. Goodspeed (Chicago 1956).
6. *The Epistle to the Ephesians* by C. L. Milton (Oxford 1951).

# 1

## Authorship, destination and purpose
## Eph 1:1–2

The very first word of this epistle provides one of the most perplexing problems of biblical scholarship. If Paul was really the author of this epistle, then there are a number of questions which demand some kind of answer.

The literary style of the letter differs greatly from that of other letters of Paul and apart from the reference to Tychicus in 6:21 there are none of the usual personal greetings and comment upon local problems. In addition to this the epistle relies very heavily upon Colossians; as much as three-fifths of Ephesians is modelled very closely upon material in Colossians. A table of parallel passages is given in the appendix.

The theological and ethical ideas are often said to indicate a later date. The theology of the church, for example, is much more developed here than elsewhere in Paul and it is obvious that the second coming of Christ is no longer regarded as of central importance.

Defenders of Pauline authorship argue that Paul's own ideas may have developed in these directions and that other difficulties may be explained by the special character of the letter. There is no space to go very deeply into the question here but it is obvious that the problem is highly complex. Only by considering the exact character of the letter can we get any nearer to an answer.

In some manuscripts the second part of verse one reads 'to the saints who are at Ephesus and faithful to Christ Jesus'. This reading is not found in the most reliable manuscripts but it is the only explicit link between this epistle and the church at Ephesus. One explanation is that this letter was intended as a round robin to be circulated throughout Asia Minor. It might have been written at the same time as Colossians and been delivered to various churches en route by Tychicus. This would account for the similarities with Colossians, the absence of personal greetings and some of the differences of style.

Another suggestion is that this letter was written by a disciple of Paul who intended it as a systematic elaboration of Paul's theology brought up to date for the needs of christians living at the end of the apostolic era. According to the standards of the time this kind of claim would not have been regarded as dishonest. Indeed it would have been thought very praiseworthy for a disciple to write a document under his dead master's name.

More recently some scholars have suggested that Ephesians may consist largely of liturgical material in use in the Ephesian church. 1:3–14, 2:1–22 and 3:14–21 form what may have been a continuous thanksgiving prayer based on Jewish thanksgiving prayers used at the feast of Pentecost. J. C. Kirby in his excellent *Ephesians, Baptism and Pentecost* develops this idea very convincingly and tries to show that Ephesians was originally a baptismal liturgy, later mistakenly regarded as a letter from Paul. Acceptance of Kirby's theory will be presupposed by much of what is being offered as commentary for this discussion outline. Unfortunately there is no room here to do justice either to Kirby's analysis or to possible

objections to it. In any case, as Kirby himself remarks at
the conclusion of his essay, 'the enigma of Ephesian remains'. The most he can claim is that his theory leaves
fewer questions unanswered than other theories advanced
so far.

*If this letter was not written by Paul does it undermine
the belief that the bible is divinely inspired?*

# 2

# The new brotherhood
# Eph 1:3–3:21

**Eph 1:3–14. First thanksgiving**

The style of 1:3–14 reads rather more like a hymn or a prayer than part of a letter. If the second person plural in verse twelve is changed to the first person plural then all fourteen verses can be seen as one composition setting out the contents for the whole epistle. The theme of these verses can be laid out under a variety of headings, but can most easily be set down as follows:

> Praise of God (3) and of his gracious plan (4–6); the grace of God experienced as forgiveness (6–7), and as a revelation: this revelation is directed towards the unity of all things (9 and 10) and is shared by all christians (11–12) including the readers themselves (13–14).

The structure is so like that of the *berakah*, or Jewish thanksgiving, that some scholars regard the prayer as a part of a primitive eucharistic prayer, perhaps associated with a service of baptism. Each of the verses in this section is closely paralleled by prayers used in synagogue services. For example, verses 2 and 3 have strong echoes in the Jewish benediction 'Blessed are you, O Lord God, king of the universe. Blessed are you, O Lord, who are gracious and have chosen your people Israel in love'. A full table of such parallels can be found in Kirby's book, page 133. 1:20-23, 2:4-10 and 14-18 all partake of this character.

1:3 links up with 1:2 with the repetitive words 'God', 'Father', and 'Lord Jesus Christ'. The idea that God has blessed us 'in Christ . . . in the heavenly places' suggests that the christian already shares in the risen life of the ascended and glorified Christ. Perhaps too the readers are meant to notice a contrast with the earthly blessings promised under the old covenant (see, for example, Deut 28:1-14).

The word 'choose' in 1:4 emphasises the entirely gratuitous character of God's relationship with the believing community and this choice is made through the eternal Christ in accordance with an eternal plan. The uniting of the words 'holy and blameless' indicate that man's response to God's plan is not simply one of ritual purity but of moral goodness. This was, of course, the message of the prophets and is found in the best traditions of judaism. To be 'holy and blameless' in this sense meant being God's 'sons' practising the same loving obedience as that practised by Christ in whose risen life they now share (1:5).

The term 'beloved' in 1:6 is not found as a title of Christ anywhere else in Paul or in the new testament. It did not become current until the second century and that may have been due to the influence of this verse in Ephesians. Originally it was based on the Greek text of Is 44:2. Here it echoes and unites the ideas of the christians being destined to be sons 'in love' and in 'Jesus Christ' of the previous verse.

This eternal plan has become a historical event through the blood of Jesus shed on the cross. The word used for redemption, *apolutrosis* has the connotation of 'liberation' or 'setting free' and in the Greek text of the old testa-

ment it is used to refer to the exodus. As with the blood
of the paschal lamb the blood of Jesus marks the end of
slavery and the beginning of a new relationship with God.

The death of Christ only has liberating power to those
who are given to perceive its power (see also 1 : 17; 19,
3 : 9–10; 18 and 19). To the believers this insight is not a
'mystery' in the sense of an 'in-group' secret as in the
mystery religions. Rather it is an 'open secret'—a mystery
revealed (9). The death of Christ does not only reconcile
the individual or the church. Its ultimate purpose is the
unity and perfection of the whole universe. The Greek
word for time in 1 : 10 is not *chronos*, chronological time,
but *kairos*, the decisive 'time' that will mark the beginning of the new era. An illuminative analogy from the
world of political philosophy to help in understanding
this idea may be seen in Herbert Marcuse's discussion of
the revolutionaries shooting at the clocks during the Paris
Commune, 'thereby expressing the need that somehow
time has to be arrested and that a new time has to begin—
a very strong emphasis upon the qualitative difference
and in the totality of the rupture between the new society
and the old'. ('Liberation from the affluent Society'; essay
in *Dialectics of Liberation*, London 1968.) So too with the
fulfilment of the *kairos* when God will effect his last
revolution; the 'final rupture', 'the qualitative difference
between the new creation and the old'. One day God
'would bring everything together under Christ as head'.
This translation from the Jerusalem Bible brings out the
original meaning rather more clearly than 'unite all
things in him' (RSV). But the original Greek conveys the
idea of Christ as the principle of fulfilment and purpose
for all things. Christ sums everything up in himself and
thus foreshadows their final union and consummation.

In Christ the foundations of the revolutionary new order are already laid.

1:11–14 particularises about one aspect of the uniting of all things in Christ: the bringing together of Jews and gentiles in the church. In 11–12 the author refers to the Jews as the rightful heirs of the messianic age. Whether he is referring to Jews in general or christian Jews in particular is not completely clear. The reference to 'we who first hoped in Christ' might just conceivably be a reference to the old testament hope for the coming of the messiah. At all events the gentiles only shared in this heritage through the seal of the Holy Spirit (13). Since the whole epistle may be closely tied to the Ephesian rite of christian initiation it is interesting to note that the formula used during confirmation in the Greek church consists of the words 'The seal of the Holy Spirit'. With a characteristically Ephesian emphasis on the role of the Spirit 1:14 returns to the theme of the future inheritance as being in a sense already present.

*1. The christian believes in the future glorification and unity of all things. Should this affect the character of his involvement in society? If so, how?*

*2. How far are the author of Ephesians and modern revolutionary philosophers like Marcuse talking about the satisfaction of the same kind of need and hope in man? Are their approaches mutually exclusive? To what extent?*

## Eph 1:15–23. A prayer for the readers of the epistle

The style now reverts to that of a letter although it soon breaks back into the splendidly stylised language of a *berakah*. In content it is a prayer for the readers but like many Jewish prayers it is an intercession that begins with thanksgiving (1:16). Consistent with the much more developed trinitarian understanding in this epistle the author prays that the Father, 'the God of our Lord Jesus Christ' will give them 'a spirit of wisdom' (17) so that they may understand the character both of their christian hope (18) and of the power of God who raised Jesus from the dead and exalted him over all creation. This 'fulness', or completeness of Christ is now communicated to his body the church (22).

Verses 15 to 17 seem to be copied from Colossians 1:3 and 4. In any case 1:16 provides problems for those scholars who try to maintain that Paul wrote this letter to the church at Ephesus since Paul would have had first-hand knowledge of the quality of the faith of the church at Ephesus and would not have had to rely upon hearsay. Only in verse 17 do we find God referred to as either 'Father of glory' or 'God of our Lord Jesus Christ'. This second title was made use of by the arians in the fourth century to show that Jesus was not of equal divinity with the Father. The orthodox writers replied by suggesting that the verse referred only to the God of Jesus' humanity. In fact, of course, it was quite unfair to charge a first century writer with the task of answering fourth century questions which had never even occurred to him. Jesus himself had called the Father 'my God' (Mt 27:46) and this is the most probable basis for the use of the title here. Here, as in 3:5 and 1 Cor 2:10–12 the Spirit is seen as the source of knowledge. Whether 'spirit of wisdom' is a direct reference to the Holy Spirit is not altogether clear, although it may be taken as at least implied. Verses 17 and 18 are very like the Pentecost covenant renewal liturgy in use at Qumran, and Kirby takes this as another piece of evidence for his argument that Ephesians is a baptismal liturgy based on the Jewish service for Pentecost.

Also characteristic of Ephesians is the understanding of the place of the resurrection in the atonement. The principalities and powers, the symbols of man's estrangement from God, have been overcome not only by the death of Christ, as in Col 2:15, but by the resurrection and exaltation of Jesus. The word 'fulness' (Gk *pleroma*) in 1:23 is used a great deal in Colossians. The Colossians had come to believe in some kind of 'completeness' or fulness of God, which could only be arrived at through the agency of angelic beings. Paul had taken the term and applied it to Christ (Col 1:19). Only in Christ could this fulness of God be found. The author of Ephesians uses the term to even greater effect. Freed from the polemical undertones of its use in Colossians the word becomes an invaluable means of expressing the cosmic lordship of Christ in Ephesians, and an important stepping stone in the development of the doctrine of the divinity of Christ. Originally the word *pleroma* may have been borrowed from Greek philosophy but some scholars have claimed that much of the language used about the *pleroma* in *Ephesians* is markedly similar to that used about the concept of wisdom in the old testament; both concepts serving to mediate between creator and creature. The language of 1:23 may usefully be compared with that of Wis 7:24 and 8:1.

The doctrine of the church is far more developed in Ephesians than in the other Pauline epistles. In 1:22 and in 4:15 the church is the body and Christ the head. Elsewhere (Rom 12:4-6 and 1 Cor 12:12-13) the analogy is of each member of the church as a member of the body as a whole. Here the church has become the body and Christ is its head. Whether 'head' means physical head or leader is as unclear in the original Greek as it is in English. Whether it is really the right translation to say that it is the church which is 'the fulness of him who fills all in all' is not completely clear from the text, but if it is then we have another contrasting point with Colossians where Paul's prayer is that the individual christian may experience the 'fulness' of Christ.

> *1. Do the fourth-century arguments over the phrase 'God of our Lord Jesus Christ' provide us with any useful guide on how not to approach scripture?*
>
> *2. If the power of evil has really been overcome (1:21) then why do we not see more evidence of Christ's lordship in the world?*

## Eph 2:1–10. The dead raised

These verses elaborate the same basic theme as in the preceding section. Prior to coming alive with Christ in baptism the converts were servants of evil and here the mythology is elaborated further than in Colossians so as to include 'the prince of the power of the air'; the word 'air' implying a status above earthly authority, but inferior to the heavenly. In this unredeemed state, 'the flesh', they were the slaves of every evil caprice (3) but in Christ they have been made alive (5) and already share in the blessings of being present with the ascended Christ (6). The 'riches of his grace' are a present reality but they will be revealed still further in the future (7). 2:8–10 asserts the characteristically Pauline emphasis upon the completely gratuitous character of God's grace.

Several aspects of the theology in this section reflect distinct developments from the teaching in the other Pauline epistles. Only in Ephesians is baptism seen as the christian's resurrection. In Romans 6:3–5, for example, baptism is the christian's death to sin and the guarantee of resurrection at the second coming of Christ. Written by Paul or not, Ephesians is clearly written later than the other epistles and there is much less emphasis here upon either the second coming or upon life after death. Redemption is seen as first and foremost a qualitative redemption here and now and there is no clear distinction made between the victory that lies in the future and the victory already achieved.

*1. Baudelaire said that the devil's cleverest ruse was to convince men that he did not exist. How literally should we take the 'prince of the power of the air'? Is it possible to take the power of evil seriously enough if we do not accept belief in a personal devil?*

*2. What are the advantages and/or disadvantages of thinking of personal resurrection mainly as a present reality rather than as a future hope?*

*3. In what ways can bad religious education give the impression that man's salvation is his 'own doing' and based on works?*

## Eph 2:11–22. Reconciliation of Jew and gentile

These verses deal with the sharing by the gentiles in the salvation achieved by Christ. Through the death of Christ man is not only reconciled with God but men are reconciled with other men; more specifically, Jewish and gentile christians find that their former differences are no longer of any real significance. That this reconciliation seems to be taken as an accepted fact leads some scholars to see evidence here for a later date for the epistle after the death of Paul, when the controversies between Jewish and gentile christians had lost some of their edge.

2:12 is very like Col 1:21, although here the words 'estranged . . . in mind' become 'alienated from the commonwealth of Israel'. The reference to the blood of Christ in 2:13 refers to the death of Christ but may also involve the symbolism of the blood shed in proselyte circumcision. The 'dividing wall' refers to the partition that prevented non-Jews from entering those parts of the temple beyond the court of the gentiles. As in Col 2:14 the abolition of the law is seen as integral to Christ's act of redemption (15). The reconciliation of Jew and gentile is located in Christ's body, the church (16) and verse 17 offers a unique and, one must observe, very non-Pauline emphasis upon the reconciling function of the preaching of Christ (a reference to Is 52:7 and 19). 2:18 is another excellent example of the trinitarian emphasis in Ephesians. Neither the idea of 'access . . . to the Father' nor approaching him 'in the Spirit' are found elsewhere in Paul. The metaphor for the church in 2:19–22 now becomes that of a temple —an analogy perhaps suggested by the image of the 'dividing wall' in 2:14. The church in Ephesians is not the local church of the other Pauline epistles but the universal church, the growing human community of those who are built into the same structure with Christ and with each other.

*1. If the death of Christ is really about the breaking down of barriers between people, how can we account for the existence of christians who accept racism or support an economic system which separates people along lines of class or colour?*

*2. How can christian teachers and preachers best recover this emphasis on the social implications of the death of Christ?*

## Eph 3:1–13. The place of Paul in God's plan

These thirteen verses are an interruption in the development of the argument of the epistle and their style differs sharply from that of the sonorous and highly stylised liturgical language which precedes it. Written more or less in parenthesis these verses constitute an eulogy of Paul for his role in God's 'economy' or plan.

3:1–6 are clearly based upon Col 1:23–27 and 3:1, like Col 1:23, makes a fairly emphatic claim to Pauline authorship. Apparently Paul is writing from prison and sees his imprisonment as a matter for some pride since imprisonment is one of the signs of a true apostle (2 Cor 11:23). Paul accepts his imprisonment as something to be endured both for Christ and for his gentile converts. The 'revelation' referred to may well be a reference to his conversion on the road to Damascus (Ac 9:1–6 and Gal 1:16). By this, or some subsequent revelation, his readers should be able to realise his insight into 'the mystery of Christ'. The mystery of Christ has always been dimly perceived by men of other times but it is now revealed to the 'holy apostles and prophets'. 3:6 seems to refer back to Paul's insight into this mystery in 3:4. His insight into the mystery of Christ is what enabled him to perceive that the gentiles were called to be 'partakers of the promise in Christ Jesus'.

It is often claimed that the phrase 'holy apostles and prophets' is too deferential to have been written by Paul and sounds much more like a writer of the next generation to whom the apostles were much larger than life. This is not a conclusive argument however. 'Holy' simply means 'set apart' and can be used of any christian. The 'prophets' referred to here are the prophets of the christian church rather than of the old testament and the word 'apostles' may be being used loosely to refer, not just to the twelve, but to a general category of missionaries.

The self-deprecating tone of 3:8 is very like 1 Cor 15:9 and is used to emphasise how much Paul owes to God's grace and power (3:7). Paul had been called to preach Christ to the gentiles and to enable them to see that the church, the believing community, is a sign to the 'principalities and powers' (11). The hag-ridden estranged condition of man has been radically altered and believers have free access to the Father (12). With this in mind Paul's readers are exhorted not to be anxious about him.

*Do you agree that we should expect preachers of the gospel to be persecuted and imprisoned like Paul? Where they are not being persecuted and imprisoned, is this because they are failing in their task or because the secular authorities have become more christian?*

## Eph 3:14–21. Conclusion of thanksgiving prayer

The 'reason I bow my knees' almost certainly refers back to 3:13. The Father is adored for incorporating the readers as stones in the building of the temple. The standing position for prayer was the normal posture in the early church and falling upon his knees means that the writer was quite overcome by a sense of urgency and intense emotion. In the church the christian finds brotherhood with Christ and sonship with the Father and this provides the model and goal for every human social unit. The word for family in 3:15 is *patria* and is etymologically linked with *pater*: father. 3:16–17 are among the most beautiful in the new testament. The Spirit is seen as a source of strength to the 'inner man'. This phrase does not refer to the intellectual or any other part of a man but to that part of his personality which is spiritual: the part of his character that has already been redeemed.

3 : 18 refers to the four dimensions of breadth, length, height and depth. Usually this image is attributed to the influence of stoic philosophy but it may be traceable to some of the language used about wisdom in the old testament (see Job 28 : 12–14 and 21–22; Sir 1 : 2–3, 24 : 28–29 and Wis 9 : 16–17). As in the wisdom literature the language used expresses both the remoteness and the nearness of God. The God of the bible is both more transcendent and more immanent than the God of the stoics, whose conception of God was rather crudely pantheistic.

In 3 : 19 the love of Christ is referred to as above knowledge; meaning that it is a more profound intimation of reality than anything to be gained either through speculative philosophy or semi-pagan mystery religions. The fruit of this knowledge is to be filled with the fulness (*pleroma*) of God.

The section ends with a doxology and an *Amen* which strengthen the impression that much of the first three chapters are part of a liturgical thanksgiving, possibly a eucharistic prayer.

*1. Can you suggest any reasons why we might find it somewhat daunting 'to know the love of Christ which surpasses knowledge?' Ought we not, in any case, to be suspicious of any truth which is not logically deducible from reason alone?*

*2. Do you consider that the kneeling position for prayer should be used only exceptionally? What advantages are attributed to the standing position in the modern liturgical movement?*

*3. The idea of God as a Father (3:14–15) is clearly only an analogy. Are there any psychologically harmful ways of thinking of God as a Father? How can they be avoided?*

# 3
## Appeal to unity
## Eph 4:1–32

### Eph 4:1–3. The bond of peace

The section opens by referring again to Paul's captivity. The readers of the letter should be moved by Paul's sufferings to practise all the humility, gentleness and patience which is necessary for the maintenance of the unity of the Spirit. The baptised christian is in a new relationship with every other baptised christian whatever natural differences may exist between them. As John Chrysostom expressed it, 'The Spirit unites those who are separated by race and customs'. When Jews meet they recognise each other with the beautiful greeting *shalom*, meaning 'peace'. Through their common faith and heritage each Jew is in 'the bond of peace' with every other Jew. Christian brotherhood in the Spirit represents an even wider 'bond of peace', the *shalom* into which all men are now being called.

*Do you agree that the divisions between christians seriously impair the church's witness to Christ? Are the most serious divisions found in the existence of separate denominations or in the differences which exist within individual denominations? How much danger is there of work for christian unity becoming inward looking and irrelevant to the real problem of the church's relationship with the modern world?*

## Eph 4:4–6. The basis of christian unity

Using language which echoes that used in the first three chapters, the author examines the sevenfold basic structure of christian unity: body, Spirit, hope, Lord, faith, baptism, one God and Father. Christians are called to be one visible community, 'one body', and the Spirit is the invisible principle of this community inspiring its members to a closer unity. They are sustained by the 'one hope'; acknowledge the 'one Lord', Jesus Christ, confess the 'one faith' and they are all sharers in the 'one baptism'. Above all, their unity is implied in the unity of God the Father who is himself both omnipresent and transcendent. The ascending order of Spirit, Lord and Father illustrate the highly developed trinitarian emphasis of this epistle.

*Does the phrase 'one faith' imply an agreed set of dogmas? How much doctrinal agreement is necessary before two denominations enter into full communion with each other?*

## Eph 4:7–16. Using God's gifts for the whole church

Having dealt with the basic principles of unity the epistle goes on to discuss the importance of diversity in the life of the church. 4:7 echoes Rom 12:6 'Having gifts that differ according to the grace given to us . . .' and 1 Cor 12:4 'there are varieties of gifts but the same Spirit'. In this case, however, the writer is talking about the ministries in the church as a whole rather than in particular local churches.

In 4:8 the writer bases his argument upon Ps 68:18 which he is either quoting inaccurately or else drawing from some version which no longer exists. In its original sense the verse referred to Yahweh bringing the Israelites out of captivity in Egypt, although later Jewish writers applied the verse to Moses going up into Sinai and returning with the commandments ('You ascended to the firmament, O prophet Moses, you took captivity captive, you taught the words of the law, you gave gifts to the sons of men'). The feast of Pentecost commemorated the giving of the law and this psalm was used in the synagogue service on that day. Not surprisingly the verse is applied to Jesus as the new Moses and the Holy Spirit as the chief gift of the risen Christ. The notion of Jesus returning triumphant with prisoners of war is much more vividly expressed in Col 2:15 where the prisoners are specified as the elemental spirits, the principalities and powers.

4:9–10 emphasises the idea of the incarnation as a prelude to the ascension when Jesus took in his full cosmic role as the 'fulness' of all things. 'Lower parts of the earth' has also been taken to refer to Christ's 'descent into the realm of the dead' between Good Friday and Easter day.

The list of gifts or charisms which flow from the Spirit are all linked here with teaching roles in the church and there is no mention of any ministry in connection with healing or the gift of tongues (see 1 Cor 12:27–31).

All these gifts have the practical function of 'building up the body of Christ'. Through the various teaching ministries there is a continual movement towards unity of faith, knowledge of Christ and spiritual maturity measuring up to 'the stature of the fulness of Christ'. Not everything childlike is a christian virtue (14) and the vacillating quality of childhood is seen as a serious danger to the unity of faith. The real defence against false teaching is seen as lying in close co-operation between all the members of the body and in the love that binds them together

(15). It is this love which enables the christian to use his gifts for the benefit of the whole community.

*1. What new forms of christian ministry are appropriate in the church today?*

*2. Is there any point in talking about 'heresies' today? How could they be recognised?*

## Eph 4:17–24. Two differing life-styles

At this point the baptised are solemnly conjured and exhorted ('I affirm and testify in the Lord') to reject the life style of the society among whom they lived. The word 'gentile' refers here to any unconverted person. Such persons were in a fallen condition characterised by darkened understanding and hardness of heart; that is to say by an ignorance that proceeded, in part at least, from malice. This ignorance was the root cause of pagan sexual depravity (see also Rom 1:21–32). In baptism, however, the christian has gained an entirely new perspective upon the moral life (20). The life style revealed in Jesus contrasts very markedly with this pagan life style. In baptism the convert 'put off' this life style with his old clothes before he went down into the font to be renewed. The acceptance of a new life style was symbolised by the putting on of the baptismal garment when he had come up out of the water.

*1. Is there any real conflict between the attitude taken to 'ignorance' in 4:18 and the ecumenical tolerance we are encouraged to adopt today?*

*2. What constitutes sexual impurity and to what extent is any definition affected by changing social attitudes?*

## Eph 4:25–32. Further contrasts

This epistle does not limit christian moral renewal to sexual morality, but suggests further contrasts; between falsehood and truth (25); righteous and unrighteous anger (26–27); stealing and working for others (28); evil talk and edifying (29). The section ends with a further list of six vices: bitterness, wrath, anger, clamour, slander, and malice (37). Against these the author sets kindness, tenderness, and forgiveness (38).

Some of the vices in these verses deserve special explanation. 'Falsehood' in 25 is a more comprehensive idea than 'lying' and suggests a total absence of sincerity. The 'evil talk' in 29 is similarly comprehensive and does not refer to any one particular line of bad conversation. In verse 31 'bitterness' refers to a state of irreconcilable resentment. 'Wrath and anger', almost synonymous in English, refer to different types of anger. 'Wrath' refers to a sudden flaring up; 'anger' to a smouldering rage.

None of the vices listed here are presented simply as a code to be observed either under pain of punishment or in hope of a reward. The baptised person must be sincere and truthful because he belongs to the other members of the body (25). The thief should work in order to have money to support the poor (28). Scurrilous talk should be abandoned in favour of conversation that will be helpful to others so as not to sadden the Spirit received in baptism (29–30). Above all christian love and forgiveness should flow directly from a sense of loving gratitude for one's redemption in Christ (32).

*1. Is the positive and non-mercenary approach to christian morality a suitable approach for christian education?*

*Does the negative and mercenary approach have a place with the morally and spiritually immature?*

2. *To what degree is the positive approach already predominant among christians?*

3. *Is truthfulness always practicable? For example, could one possibly ask every christian politician or salesman to always be sincere?*

4. *What constitutes evil talk and why?*

# 4

# The imitation of God
# Eph 5:1–6:23

### Eph 5:1–20. The basis of christian morality

These verses continue with the general principles of christian morality which the author has began to outline in the previous chapter. The author is taking the six last, more immediately social, of the ten commandments and using them as convenient pegs on which to hang his theme of the contrast between christian and non-christian conduct. Elaboration on the commandment not to kill, not to steal and not to bear false witness had been given in 4:26, 28 and 29. In 5:3–5 he develops his teaching on the commandments not to covet or commit adultery. In 5:1–2 the author returns to the theme of 4:32, that the conduct of christian life is one of direct response to God's love in Christ. To be God's beloved children means to imitate the perfection of God just as children imitate the qualities of their parents. The words 'fragrant offering and sacrifice' suggest technical terms for sacrifice in the old testament. To live a life based on love involves becoming a sacrificial offering like Christ.

In this verse the self-offering of Christ is not explicitly identified with his death. In passing we might suggest that the importance of the cross can never be seen in isolation from his whole life. The acceptance of his Father's will, even at the moment of physical and psychological destruc-

203

tion, served as the climax of a life of loving obedience but it is very difficult for us to believe that God was specially pleased or placated by suffering and death as such. Rather, suffering and death served as vehicles of total trust, love and obedience.

'Let no one deceive you with empty words' is a reference to false teachers, probably the type of teachers who had threatened the faith of the Colossians. 'Once you were darkness' refers to the christian condition prior to being enlightened by baptism. Through baptism the christian receives the knowledge and power to rise above the petty vices and degradations which characterise man in his unredeemed condition. The similarity between these verses and passages in John's gospel (12:35–6 and 3:20–21) may just be fortuitous, but some scholars see them as evidence that both writers are drawing from the same Ephesian tradition. The metaphor of 'children of light' combating the darkness comes originally from the Dead Sea sect at Qumran. The exposing of the 'unfruitful works of darkness' (11) does not exclude verbal reproof but is best understood in the light of 5:13. The virtuous life of the christian serves as a living reproof to everything that falls short of it.

5:14 is almost certainly a verse from a primitive baptismal liturgy and links the metaphor of dying and rising with the metaphor of light and darkness.

The content of 5:15–19 follows 4:5 and 3:16–17. The antitheses of wisdom and foolishness are now added to those of light and darkness, dead and risen. The christian must act out of a sense of urgency (16) and conform to the will of God as revealed in Christ (17). 5:18 contrasts two kinds of intoxication; the one attributable to alcohol, the other to the Holy Spirit (see also Ac 2:13). The intoxicating effects of wine were much valued in pagan mysteries and religions, but the joy of the christian assembly does not need to be artificially induced, and verse nineteen vividly portrays the exuberantly festive character of the meetings in the early church. The Greek for 'giving thanks' is *eucharistountes*: for the christian the whole of life becomes one great eucharist to the Father in the name of Christ. The phrase 'in the name of our Lord Jesus Christ' is a deliberate alteration of Col 3:17 which has 'giving thanks to God the Father through him'. In Colossians and elsewhere Paul uses the word 'through' in this context and many scholars urge this verse as clear evidence that Paul did not write Ephesians. The phrase 'in the name' may of course be another clue to the connection between the epistle and baptism. In Acts (2:38, 8:16 and 10:48) we read of baptism 'in the name of' the Lord Jesus (whether this was actually the more primitive formula is not entirely clear). In this verse of Ephesians we probably have an exhortation to the newly baptised to translate the reality of their baptism into a lifetime of thankfulness.

*1. Do you agree that a too crude understanding of the sacrifice of Christ might lead to a distorted idea of God?*

*2. Should christians associate themselves with movements for the tightening of censorship? Is example better than precept in matters of sexual ethics? Do you agree with those who see sinister and totalitarian undertones in movements like 'moral rearmament', or in events like the 'festival of light' which took place in London in 1971?*

*3. When does the use of alcohol or other drugs become a substitute for the Holy Spirit? What different attitudes do christians have towards drink and why?*

*4. Are the ten commandments always a useful basis for moral teaching?*

## Eph 5:21–33. Marriage and the love of Christ for the church

The author goes on to give specific moral teaching. Brides, children and slaves are all to practise subjection (5:21, 6:1 and 6:5). Husbands, parents and slave owners are to be loving to their subjects. The sociological structure of these relationships is, of course, completely alien to us. In our society wives aim to be equal, slavery is considered abhorrent and if children are still expected to be subject to their parents there is at least a very different and more permissive kind of relationship between children and parents now than existed in the first century AD. The essential message, however, is the same and can be translated into any social context; that human relationships should be based upon love and mutual respect.

The principle of the wife's subjection to her husband is thoroughly Pauline and had already been developed more fully in 1 Cor 11. If justice is to be done, however, there is no point at all in comparing the role of the wife described here with that of a middle-class wife in Britain or America today. By the standards of all contemporary cultures and most subsequent ones, these verses represent a charter of women's liberation! At all events, the submissive wife is seen as a splendid simile for the vocation of the christian community; knowing that it is loved, the church can be like a submissive bride who has absolute confidence in her husband.

Marriage is here seen in terms of sexual union involving such a degree of self-giving and intimacy that the husband and wife become like one physical entity. The words in 5:31 are a quotation from Gen 2:24 and recall the myth of Eve's creation from Adam's rib. Through loving sexual union man and woman receive their sense of completeness in each other. The husband can experience the feeling that his wife's body is not an alien object but part of himself. All this contrasts markedly with Paul's less positive attitude to marriage in 1 Cor 7 and may represent yet another item of evidence against the Pauline authorship of Ephesians.

This picture of marriage provides the author with his third metaphor for the church. In 1:22-23, 2:16, 3:6 and 4:15-16 the church is the body and Christ the head. In 2:20-22 and 4:12 the church is the building and Christ the cornerstone. Here Christ is the bridegroom. The idea of God's covenant with his people being like a marriage recurs throughout the old testament and is found in Hosea, Amos, Jeremiah, Isaiah and Ezekiel. As with Yahweh's bathing of his bride in Ez 16:9, Christ bathes his church (26); a clear reference to baptism, and 'with the word' probably refers to the baptismal formula 'I baptise you. . . .'

5:27 points to the eschatological character of the church's perfection. In Col 1:28 it is the individual christian who is presented to the Father. In 2 Cor 11:2 it is the Corinthian church that is presented as a bride to Christ. In this verse it is the universal church, not just as she is, but as she will be, when she will be presented to the Father as the spotless bride of Christ. By 5:32 the whole analogy is getting a bit strained. It is all a 'mystery' however: a long hidden secret now revealed. It is emphasised that the observations about marriage are not the long hidden secret. Presumably this kind of perspective is always available to people of genuine love and sensibility. The real mystery is the loving union which exists between Christ and the church.

*1. Is there a specifically christian sexual morality? Why*

should we use this passage in support of the christian ideal of sexual love within marriage and ignore it on the point of woman's subjection to man?

2. What attitude do you take to those who argue that sexual union can still be beautiful, fulfilling and unselfish, even when a man and woman are not totally committed (eg do not necessarily intend to marry)?

3. Does 'become one' simply mean that intercourse has taken place after a properly witnessed ceremony or does it imply something deeper? What relevance does this question have for the problem of the broken marriage?

4. What are the dangers of regarding the institutional church as a perfect society now?

## Eph 6:1–9. Instruction in child-parent and slave-master relationships

In these verses the teaching of Col 3:18–4:1 is expanded and given a more positive and community-orientated approach. Here as elsewhere the differences can be taken either as evidence against Pauline authorship or as an indication of the special circumstances of this letter. Parents and children now have mutual obligations 'in the Lord'. Slave–master relationships were not in the Lord but 'as to Christ'. The common bond of baptism was seen as underwriting family ties. The institution of slavery, on the other hand, was tolerated rather than defended.

Scholars have argued over whether 6:1 indicates that children were baptised in the early church. Clearly the author is regarding them as members of it, although 1 Cor 7:14 has been taken to mean that children of believers did not require baptism but were already 'holy'. However, since this whole section is probably an exhortation to the newly baptised it is hard not to conclude that some of those being addressed are baptised children (although we do not know how old they were).

6:6 introduces the fourth commandment, the last of the six commandments to be discussed. All family relationships are now to be lived in Christ; the obligation of this commandment is not all on the side of the children.

The instructions to slaves and their masters provides an interesting comparison with Col 3:24–25, where the prospects of divine reward and punishment are referred to as sound reasons for following Paul's advice. Here the motive appealed to is that slaves and masters are both really equal in the sight of God.

*1. What are the extent and limits of the obedience children owe to parents? How far are our duties modified by changes in society?*

*2. Should we be scandalised that christians did not immediately oppose the institution of slavery? Do we tolerate equivalent scandals today?*

## Eph 6:10–23. The holy war

The moral teaching now moves back from the particular to the general. Husbands and wives; parents and children; slaves and master; each has a specific role to play but every christian is called to the same fierce conflict; a holy war against the forces of darkness. This theme of spiritual warfare is a particular theme of the Pauline literature and may be found in 1 Thess 5:8, 2 Cor 6:7 and 10:4 and in Rom 13:12. As in the Qumran writings, religious faith is seen in terms of a fight to the death with the forces of darkness. Christians are seen metaphorically as soldiers holding their ground in a hand-to-hand battle against 'the wiles of the devil'. Only in Ephesians and the pastoral epistles is the word 'devil' used. Elsewhere in the Pauline literature the word 'Satan' is employed.

6:12 develops the mythology still further. The Greek word for 'world rulers' is sometimes used of kings but here it clearly indicates the angelic beings who were thought to control the world. St Jerome who, even as a hermit in the desert, was tortured by the recollection of voluptuous young women, understood that this verse referred to the struggle with 'the flesh' in the sense of sexual desire, but this interpretation tells us more about St Jerome than about the meaning of the text.

The 'evil day' in 6:13 might be taken to mean the last judgement or the final rule of the evil power just before the last day. Alternatively, it may be taken to refer simply to the present, the time when evil forces still have some power. Each of the items of armour in 6:14–17 refer to an item of armour or clothing as worn by the Roman legionaries. Each item is given a symbolic meaning but the exact symbolism ought not to be pressed too closely. The same analogy is used in Is 59:17 and Wis 5:17–20, where it is applied to God, and in Is 11:4 where it is applied to the messiah.

6:18 is the only place in the Pauline epistles where we read of praying 'in the Spirit'. Elsewhere it is the Spirit who is himself the source of the prayer. 6:19 underlines the close relationship between prayer and mission. This verse is obviously based on Col 4:3 and is one more instance of a verse that has been either altered or misunderstood by the author of Ephesians.

Verses 19 and 20 clearly refer to Paul's life and are two of the six verses which would have had to have been added if the epistle was originally a liturgical text.

Tychicus (21–22) is referred to in Col 4:7–8 and this had led some scholars to suppose that this epistle was originally the letter to the Laodiceans referred to there. The nineteenth-century liberal protestant Adolf Harnack suggested that this title was dropped when the Church of Laodicea fell into disgrace (Rev 3:14f). 'Peace' and 'grace' in verses 23 and 24 are in the reverse order from the usual Pauline usage.

*1. How would you explain these verses to someone who did not believe in evil spirits? What is the real nature of the christian conflict today?*

*2. What part does intercessory prayer play in the missionary activity of the church? Is there a case for purely contemplative orders?*

# Appendix
# Parallel passages with Colossians

If these references are studied carefully readers will be able to appreciate the extent of the dependence of Ephesians on Colossians. The differences, some of which have been discussed in the commentary, are often more instructive than the similarities.

| *Eph* | | *Col* |
|---|---|---|
| 1:7 | Freedom and forgiveness of sins in Christ | 1:14 |
| 1:10 | Everything in heaven and earth | 1:20 |
| 1:15–17 | The faith of the readers prompts Paul to give thanks and to pray for them | 1:34 |
| 1:18 | The christian hope | 1:27 |
| 1:21 | Christ superior to the principalities and powers | 1:16 |
| 1:22–23 | The church the body of Christ | 1:18–19 |
| 2:5 | Dead made alive in Christ | 2:13 |
| 2:12 | Strangers and aliens | 1:21 |
| 2:15 | Law abolished by death of Christ | 2:14 |
| 2:16–17 | Peace through the cross | 1:20 |
| 3:1 | Paul's sufferings | 1:24 |
| 3:2 | Paul's ministry | 1:25 |
| 3:3 | The mystery made known | 1:26 |

| Eph | | Col |
|---|---|---|
| 3:7 | Paul minister of the mystery | 1:23 |
| 3:8 | Paul to preach the riches of Christ to the gentiles | 1:27 |
| 3:9 | Mystery hidden for ages | 1:26 |
| 4:1 | Readers asked to lead a life worthy of the Lord | 1:10 |
| 4:2 | Catalogue of christian virtues | 3:12–14 |
| 4:3 | Unity and peace | 3:14–15 |
| 4:15 | Growth in the body of Christ | 2:19 |
| 4:19 | Pagan vices | 3:5 |
| 4:22–24 | Putting on a new nature in baptism | 3:8–10 |
| 4:25 | Truthfulness and other virtues | 3:8–9 |
| 4:29 | Evil talk | 3:8, 4:6 |
| 4:31 | Further vices | 3:8 |
| 4:32 | Mutual forbearance and forgiveness | 3:12–13 |
| 5:3 | Vices to be abandoned | 3:5 |
| 5:4 | Further vices to be abandoned | 3:8 |
| 5:5 | The true nature of idolatry | 3:5 |
| 5:6 | The wrath of God | 3:6 |
| 5:15 | Making the most of the time | 4:5 |
| 5:19 | Psalms and hymns and spiritual songs | 3:16 |
| 5:20 | Giving thanks to God | 3:17 |
| 5:22 | Wives subject to husbands | 3:18 |
| 5:25 | Husbands to love wives | 3:19 |
| 6:1 | Children to obey parents | 3:20 |
| 6:4 | Fathers not to provoke children | 3:21 |
| 6:5 | Slaves to be obedient | 3:22 |
| 6:9 | Masters to be just to slaves | 4:1 |
| 6:18 | Prayer at all times | 4:2 |
| 6:19 | Prayer requested for writer | 4:6 |
| 6:20 | Writer in prison | 4:7 |
| 6:21 | Reference to Tychicus | 4:7 |